LONDON PRECINCTS

A curated guide to the city's best shops, eateries, bars and other hangouts

LONDON PRECINCTS

A curated guide to the city's best shops, eateries, bars and other hangouts

FIONA McCARTHY

hardie grant publishing

CONTENTS

London is a big city. There's no rhyme or rhythm to the street patterns, unlike New York, and there's little of the expansive, wide, airy boulevards of Paris. Everything is a hodge podge of ideas, too many building sites, and diverse and iconic architecture – some of it centuries old and so beautiful it stops you in your tracks. There are crazy people, rattling black cabs, cyclists zipping through streets never designed to cope with so much traffic; and, of course, every ethnicity and culture on the planet, happily rubbing alongside each other.

It's this diversity that enriches every Londoner's daily life and brings out some endearing quirks. While the Brits enjoy bemoaning the weather (although it really doesn't rain half as much as everyone says it does, honest), they're also very good at saying sorry (even when it's you who's bumped into them). They queue in neat orderly lines with never a thought to pushing in. And even though they're often reluctant to make eye contact on the Tube, they'll quite happily chat away to you on the bus.

When I travel, I plan my day around visiting a key cultural spot and then work out what else there is to see nearby, so I've taken a similar approach with this book. London has it all – luxury designer shops, Michelin-starred restaurants, groovy cafes, amazing high street shopping, the Royal family! With so much to include, I've focused mostly on the things that feel distinctively British, and I have no doubt you can work out the rest simply by wandering around this big, beautiful city. Do plan ahead, though, if there's a play or exhibition you want to see or a special afternoon tea or dinner you want to try – it's a busy city and places get booked out.

I've lived in London for more than 20 years and I've walked almost every inch of it as a freelance writer and stylist – I've been so lucky to have access to buildings usually closed to the outside world and to meet the city's best chefs, designers, shopkeepers and artisans. And I still don't feel I know everything about the capital, and I doubt I ever will.

Fiona McCarthy

There's too much to do in a day in London, so if I could eulogise over the perfect day in this beautiful city, I would break it down into dream scenarios.

On a sunny day, I would start with a long walk from home, venturing along the leafy-lined Grand Western Canal to the basin at **Little Venice** (it's the spot to catch the **London Waterbus** for an idyllic cruise down Regent's Canal with stop-offs at **London Zoo** and **Camden Lock**). From here, walking via the Westway underpass to Paddington, I'd keep heading south, in the direction of Hyde Park but then detour left to Connaught Street for coffee and delicious cake, served on pretty plates at **Cocomaya**; a window browse of the gems at **De Roemer**; the sweet indie-label fashions in **Viola**; and glittery heels at **Lucy Choi**, Jimmy Choo's niece. From here it's a quick walk, via the fountains at Marble Arch, to Mayfair and the West End. There's always a great exhibition at the **Royal Academy** (*see* page 142) or at the **National Portrait Gallery** (*see* page 068); or indulge in a pedicure (complete with head massage) at **Cowshed Carnaby**. I'd finish with a window shop through **Liberty** (*see* page 006) and **Cos** next door.

Alternatively, I might head south-west across **Hyde Park** and down Exhibition Road to the **V&A** (*see* pages 194 and 202) for the latest exhibition, a visit to the ceramics and fashion departments, coffee by the outdoor reflective pool and a browse around the addictive gift shop.

If I was feeling glam, a late afternoon glass of bubbles at either **Claridge's** (*see* page 150) or **The Connaught** would do the trick; or if I was in a slightly more laidback mood, I'd head for sliders and great wines by the glass at **Ham Yard Hotel** (*see* page 014). Later, I'd meet friends for dinner at **Quo Vadis** or **Hix** for generous, delicious British classics and a relaxed atmosphere; or **The Wolseley** (*see* page 162) for satisfying staples like its chicken soup with dumplings. For a special occasion, I'd book Skye Gyngell's **Spring** (*see* page 067); or Simon Rogan's Michelin-starred farm-to-fork take on British seasonality at **Fera** (and for a real treat, a spot at **Aulis**, his six-seater experimental kitchen); or **Koffmann's** for delicious updated French classics. More often, though, I love to head to the theatre – my favourites include the **Hampstead**, **National** or **Royal Court** – or a gig at the **Roundhouse** in Camden or the **Eventim Apollo** in Hammersmith.

If I was staying local, I love to meet friends for breakfast at **The Electric** (*see* page 223) or **Snaps + Rye** (*see* page 233) in Notting Hill followed by a little mooch around the markets on **Portobello Road** (*see* page 223) and **Golborne Road** (*see* page 234). I'd look in **Temperley London** (*see* page 215, I'm addicted to Alice's embroidered scarves) and have coffee and cake at **Granger & Co** on Westbourne Grove. Or I'd meet friends at **Melrose and Morgan** in Primrose Hill for delicious coffee, pastries and bowls of salads. I'd pop in for a look at the fashions at **Anna** and the homewares in **Graham & Green**; then a walk through the park to the top of **Primrose Hill** for spectacular views of London. It's not too far to walk over the railway bridge (past gorgeous lifestyle store **Tann Rokka**), down Chalk Farm Road to **Camden Stables Market** for its eclectic mix of food stalls and vintage dealers.

Sunday mornings are family time. We might head to **Tate Modern** (*see* page 130) for the latest exhibition, followed by a good pub lunch at **The Founders Arms** (*see* page 126). While I love to look at the watercolours, lincocuts and screen prints at **Bankside Gallery**, my husband and kids go down to forage on the Thames foreshore by the pub when the tide's out. **Columbia Road** market (*see* page 102) is fun too. I always have a squizz in **Nelly Duff** (*see* page 102) for emerging British artists, followed by lunch at **The Marksman** (*see* page 102). Or we'd head to any of the glorious royal parks for a lazy picnic: **Hyde Park** (*see* page 176), near the Serpentine (lake and gallery) and Princess Diana Memorial Fountain; **Regent's Park** (*see* page 020) for the playgrounds and exquisite rose gardens when in bloom; **St James's Park** (*see* page 154) for its beautiful landscaping.

For an adventure further afield, nothing beats driving very slowly (maximum speed 20 miles per hour) through **Richmond Park**, to admire the herds of deer, followed by a kitchen garden lunch at heavenly **Petersham Nurseries**, with tables set in Victorian greenhouses. Or have a good romp across **Hampstead Heath**, followed by lunch at the 16th century **Spaniards Inn**.

And if I wanted to escape for the weekend, there's nowhere better than **Babington House** in Somerset (I could disappear into its walled garden spa, never to be seen again) or **The Pig on the Beach**, overlooking Studland Bay, in Dorset.

REFUEL

RICHMOND MEWS

QUO VADIS

DEAN

BATEMAN ST

BARRAFINA

BURGER & LOBSTER

PRINCE EDWARD THEATRE

DEAN STREET TOWNHOUSE

HOPPERS

WARDOUR

MEARD STREET

FRITH

STREET

DUCKSOUP

GOSH! COMICS

BYRON BURGER

COMPTON

PETER ST

BONE DADDIES

ROMILLY STREET

OLD

STREET

THE BOX

RANDALL & AUBIN

STREET

BREWER STREET

STREET

AVENUE

TO
MAP RIGHT
(VIA BREWER STREET)

GIELGUD THEATRE

GERRARD STREET

SHAFTESBURY

RUPERT

WARDOUR

PALOMAR

LISLE

STREET

GREAT WINDMILL STREET

STREET

CAFÉ DE PARIS

STREET

WHITCOMB STREET

COVENTRY STREET

Piccadilly line

PRINCE OF WALES THEATRE

PICCADILLY CIRCUS

Bakerloo line

OXENDON STREET

JERMYN STREET

SOHO

In many ways Soho is the very heart of central London, always busy and noisy; its big neon lights around Piccadilly illuminating the sky. Soho is defined by Oxford Circus to the north, Regent Street to the west, Piccadilly Circus to the south and Leicester Square to the east.

Smart shops, coffee bars and hip restaurants are replacing the area's 20th century notoriety for naughty nightclubs, gangsters and call girls, but Soho will always have a slightly gritty edge. It's also the home of the West End theatre district – it just wouldn't be a true London experience without seeing at least one play or musical here.

24   JUN 8016

SHOP
1 CARNABY STREET
2 GOSH! COMICS
3 HAM YARD VILLAGE
SHOP AND EAT
4 LIBERTY LONDON
5 RAPHA CYCLE CLUB

17

EAT
NOPI
ASIAN CUISINE
PALOMAR
POLPO

OXFORD STREET

THE PHOTOGRAPHER'S GALLERY

EMBER YARD

STREET

NOEL

WARDOUR STREET

BERWICK

HAROLD MOORE MUSIC

PHO SOHO

WARDOUR MEWS

D'ARBLAY STREET

SISTER RAY

RECKLESS RECORDS

POLAND

PHONICA RECORDS

PORTLAND MEWS

HILLS PLACE

RAMILLIES PLACE

RAMILLIES STREET

GREAT MARLBOROUGH STREET

SOHO

WESTMINSTER

CROSSTOWN DOUGHNUTS

LIVONIA STREET

SOUNDS OF THE UNIVERSE

DUCK LANE

0 ——— 50 m

ARGYLL STREET

STREET

John Snow Water Pump

LIBERTY LONDON

PLACE

LITTLE MARLBOROUGH STREET

NEWBURGH STREET

DUFOUR'S PLACE

MARSHALL

DUCK & RICE

FOUBERT'S

CARNABY

BROADWICK

STREET

BERWICK STREET MARKET

INGESTRE

HOPKINS STREET

GANTON STREET

BAO

LEXINGTON

CARNABY STREET

KINGLY

JINJUU

PLACE

STREET

TO
GOSH! COMICS
PALOMAR,
BONE DADDIES
& GERRARD STREET
(SEE MAP LEFT)

KINGLY COURT

POLPO

UPPER JAMES STREET

GREAT PULTENEY STREET

TENISON COURT

N

BEAK

UPPER JOHN STREET

BOB BOB RICARD

BRIDLE LANE

BLACKLOCK

REGENT STREET

NOPI

Sanctum Soho Hotel

GOLDEN SQUARE

Golden Square

LOWER JAMES STREET

BREWER STREET

SMITH'S COURT

HAM YARD

Our Lady of the Assumption & Saint Gregory

MARK'S BAR AT HIX SOHO

HAM YARD BAR

HAM YARD VILLAGE

WARWICK

REGENT PLACE

LOWER JOHN STREET

SHERWOOD STREET

DENMAN STREET

Bakerloo line

STREET

BREWER

AIR

RAPHA CYCLE CLUB

EAT AND DRINK
10 Duck & Rice
11 Ham Yard Bar
12 Mark's Bar at Hix
13 Bob Bob Ricard

GLASSHOUSE

STREET

HOTEL CAFÉ ROYAL

VIGO

SACKVILLE

REGENT

STREET

PICCADILLY CIRCUS

BURLINGTON GARDENS

PICCADILLY line

Piccadilly line

JUN 8016

24

001

1.

CARNABY STREET

Carnaby Street is best known as home to 'Swinging London' of the sixties where designers like Mary Quant set up shop (and The Rolling Stones performed at the now long-gone Marquee Club a stone's throw away in Wardour Street). Today, it refers not just to the main drag but to the surrounding area that includes Kingly, Newburgh, Marshall and Beak streets and Foubert's Place. It's a particularly good spot for shopping for the boys – the Mod legacy lives on with brands such as **Lambretta**, **Ben Sherman**, **Fred Perry** and **Pretty Green** (former Oasis lead singer Liam Gallagher's fashion label). Take a trip to the barbers at **Pankhurst**, find fine British-made accessories by sixth generation tailors at **Peckham Rye**, and check out cool camera kit at **Lomography**. Trainer geeks need look no further than **Adidas Originals**, **Puma**, **Superga**, **Vans** and **Nike SB** (exclusively for skateboarders, 1st floor, 33–34 Carnaby Street). There's plenty of hip streetwear for the girls too – **Supertrash**, **Diesel**, **Cheap Monday** and **Monki**. Enjoy great coffee at **Department of Coffee and Social Affairs** (Lowndes Court) or **Urban Tearooms** (Kingly Street). For sweet tooths, try cupcakes with a twist (flavours include Mexican Hot Chocolate, Cherry Bakewell or Butterered Popcorn) from **Crumbs & Doilies** or for clean and lean, try **The Detox Kitchen** (Kingly Street).

2.

GOSH! COMICS

1 Berwick Street, W1F 0DR
020 7636 1011,
goshlondon.com
Mon–Sun 10.30am–7pm

Befitting the edgy creative energy Soho still exudes (despite the gentrification process that is slowly pushing out the sex clubs and odds-and-sods shops that made the area so unique), Gosh! Comics sprawls across two floors of street art, contemporary illustration and urban storytelling. Comics, old and new, classic and cutting-edge, fill the shelves alongside illustrated books for both adults and children; there are artworks to buy, and an ongoing series of limited-edition book plates to collect; a growing selection of its own-published books; regular artist talks and Drink & Draw nights supported by the wonderful art supply shop **Cass Art** (24 Berwick Street, W1F 8RD).

3.

HAM YARD VILLAGE

Don't miss the interesting mix of boutiques in what's dubbed Ham Yard Village – part of the courtyard surrounding Ham Yard Hotel – including the colourful resin designs by **Dinosaur Designs** (photo 3A) and **Jac + Jack**'s separates in cashmere, cotton and linen. Head to the tasting bar at **My Cup of Tea** (photo 3B) to try one of over 40 refined own-blends of tea and tisanes, gathered from around the world (there's also unusual one-off tea cups, caddies, jugs and trays for sale). Pick up Brazilian–British beachwear at **Frescobal Carioca**, admire beautiful blooms at **Bloomsbury Flowers** (photo 3D) and glamorous hand-crafted *haute joaillerie* gems at **Anabela Chan** (photo this page). Love the chic separates and cute kidswear at **Caramel** (photo 3C) and custom-designed glasses at **Eyewear Concierge**. For the very best niche fragrance, bodycare and home scent brands, head to **Brummells of London**.

3A.

2.

3B.

3C.

3D.

2.

4.

LIBERTY LONDON

Regent Street, W1B 5AH
020 7734 1234, liberty.co.uk
Mon–Sat 10am–8pm,
Sun 12–6pm

Liberty's floral Tana Lawn prints are iconic – now found on everything from the lining of a Barbour jacket to a pair of Nike trainers – as is its distinctive mock-Tudor facade. Inside, Liberty is as exotic today as when Arthur Lasenby Liberty opened it in 1875 as an Eastern-inspired bazaar of ornaments, fabrics and objets d'art. With light filtering down through the four-storey wood panelled atrium, an unexpected, often handcrafted take brings each elegant department to life – from jewellery to coats, soaps to needlepoint, plates to prints. If it all gets too deliriously dizzying, take a pitstop at **Café Liberty**, open from breakfast to afternoon tea, on the second floor – try the generous sharing platters, a hazelnut and marshmallow brownie and glass of Prosecco – before visiting its famous haberdashery department (filled with fabrics, patterns, wools and buttons). Or, from September, its magical Christmas Shop is a Santa's grotto of decorations, cards, sweets and stocking fillers!

5.

RAPHA CYCLE CLUB

85 Brewer Street, W1F 9ZN
020 7494 9831, rapha.cc
Mon–Fri 8am–8pm,
Sat 8.30am–7.30pm,
Sun 11am–6pm

Rapha Cycle Club was one of the first spots in London to combine coffee with cycles – it bustles all day with chat about the dream cycle experience and its aim is to bring together a community of passionate road riders. Alongside the full Rapha range of bike kit, track jackets, jerseys, shoes and backpacks, there are live screenings of major cycling races, and a Saturday cycle club that adventures into the countryside. The cafe provides perfect fuel for pre- and post-ride nourishment with Workshop Coffee, American pancakes, organic Scotch porridge and sandwiches inspired by racing champions – from the Freddie Grubb (Portobello mushroom, rocket and Beaufort Meule) to the Paolo Bettini (chicken, semi-dried tomatoes, watercress and olive tapenade).

6.

NOPI
21–22 Warwick Street,
W1B 5NE
020 7494 9584,
ottolenghi.co.uk/nopi
Mon–Thurs 8am–4pm &
5.30–10.30pm, Fri 8am–
10.30pm, Sat 10am–10.30pm,
Sun 10am–4pm

Famed chef Yotam Ottolenghi, with Noam Bar and Sami Tamimi, opened their first luxe deli in Notting Hill in 2002 – bowls of fresh, delicious salads, raspberry swirled meringues and decadent cakes – and turned take-away fare on its head. NOPI is a rise in the glamour stakes with glimmering, golden brass offset by a cool, white marble interior (the bathrooms, a sometimes confusing but intriguing mirrored maze), but those early Middle Eastern meets Mediterranean flavours are still here. Upstairs is more formal dining, downstairs a communal table is open all day. Feast on courgette (zucchini) and manouri fritters with cardamom yoghurt, coriander seed–crusted burrata with slices of blood orange and twice-cooked baby chicken with lemon myrtle salt and chilli jam. For dessert, NOPI's strawberry mess with sumac and rose water has fast become a classic.

7.

ASIAN CUISINE

Bao (53 Lexington Street, photos this page and 7A) is a no-frills joint no bigger than someone's squeezy sitting room, and the hour (or more) long queues outside (which originally started with a food stall in Hackney), are evidence that everyone's going crazy for their soft, pillowy Taiwanese steamed buns (cooked in milk), stuffed with fillings such as fried chicken, confit pork, daikon or lamb. If you can't bear the wait, then try nearby **Pho Soho** (Wardour Street), which is an outpost of the revered East End Vietnamese restaurant, or Korean–American chef Judy Joo's KFC (Korean Fried Chicken) at **Jinjuu** (Kingly Street), or **Bone Daddies** (Peter Street, photos 7B and 7C) ramen noodle bar. Alternatively, head south from Beak Street and across Shaftesbury Avenue, to the numerous restaurants on **Chinatown's Gerrard Street**.

7A.

7B.

7C.

PALOMAR

34 Rupert Street, W1D 6DN
020 7439 8777,
thepalomar.co.uk
Mon–Sat 12–2.30pm &
5.30–11pm, Sun 12.30–
3.30pm & 6–9pm

Prepare to immerse yourself into the madness of The Palomar, complete with chefs dancing to loud music and shots of anise-flavoured arak handed out freely to those seated at the bar. Inspired by popular restaurants like Machneyuda in Jerusalem's Mahane Yehuda market, Palomar is the current darling of the Jerusalem vibe (intermingled with Spanish and North African flavours) sweeping the London food scene. The Yemeni 'Kubaneh', a steaming pot-baked bread served with silky tahini and velvety tomatoes, is to die for; the souk-tasting deconstructed Shakshukit kebab, with minced meat, yoghurt, tahini and pita, is mandatory.

POLPO

41 Beak Street, W1F 9SB
020 7734 4479, polpo.co.uk
Mon–Sat 12–11pm, Sun
12–10pm

Polpo's 'back streets of Venice' inspired sharing dishes commanded immediate cult following when it first opened in Soho in 2009. It has since expanded to nine further venues around the city, including the highly respected **Polpetto**. Along with a bottle chosen from the well priced, carefully selected list of fresh, young Italian wines, don't miss the stuffed fried olives, spaghettini with meatballs (classic beef, spicy pork, lamb or chickpea, spinach and ricotta), and pizzettes topped with delicacies like fig and prosciutto. Finish off with an Affogato al caffè or Aperol sorbet.

8.

9.

9.

8.

8.

9.

10.

DUCK & RICE

90 Berwick Street, W1F 0QB
020 3327 7888,
theduckandrice.com
Mon–Thurs 12–11.30pm, Fri–Sat
12pm–12am, Sun 12–10.30pm

In a unique bid to create London's (and perhaps the world's) first Chinese gastro pub, Alan Yau (of Hakkasan and Yauatcha fame), has brought together oriental flavours with a micro-brewery and to-die-for interiors by Turkish designers Autoban. Gleaming copper beer tanks, harlequin-patterned stained-glass windows, handpainted blue and white tiles, swirling wrought-iron staircases and geometric-patterned dividing screens make this a visually arresting spot to linger. Downstairs, nibble on chilli and shallot cashew nuts or jasmine tea–smoked pulled rib buns, washed down with a pint of Bath Ale Gem or London Pride; upstairs feast on the Lobster Cantonese house special, crabmeat Foo Young scrambled egg, and sides of jellyfish and celery or taro, lotus root, yam bean and chilli.

11.

HAM YARD BAR

Ham Yard Hotel
1 Ham Yard, W1D 7DT
020 3642 1007,
firmdalehotels.com
Mon–Sat 7am–11.30pm,
Sun 7am–10.30pm

Ham Yard Hotel's restaurant and bar buzzes day and night as a great place for breakfast, a light lunch outside by the gleaming bronze Tony Cragg sculpture, a blow-out dinner or a quick drink and sharing plate pre- or post-theatre. The melts, sliders and 'profitabombes' are so moreish; the martini list boasts a selection of 15 vodkas, 18 gins and a dozen vermouths, and almost all wines are available by the glass. The vibrant, eclectic interior kaleidoscope of colour, pattern, art and neon (designed by Kit Kemp) is what makes this hotel so special. Take a tour downstairs to see the voluminous Dive Bar and the 1950s bowling alley and groovy Croc nightclub; then go up to the fourth floor garden for fantastic views across Soho's rooftops.

12.

MARK'S BAR AT HIX SOHO

66–70 Brewer Street, W1F 9UP
020 7292 3518, marksbar.co.uk
Mon–Fri 12–11.30pm,
Sat 11am–11.30pm, Sun
12–10.30pm

- -

Chef Mark Hix is an avid champion of all things British, whether it's the art on the walls (Damien Hirst, Tracey Emin, Harland Miller, et al.) or the distinctive ingredients he uses in his dishes – devilled chicken hearts, fresh Cornish oysters, his own home-smoked salmon, Somerset apple brandy. There's nowhere better than disappearing downstairs into the cosy, leather-sofa, smoky-hued ambience of Mark's Bar where you can play billiards as you sip on an apothecary-inspired cocktail (like a Fizz-Ness, with plum infused Tanqueray London dry gin, chamomile syrup, honey water, egg white and lemon) and nibble on peas fresh out of their pods or pork crackling dipped in Bramley apple sauce.

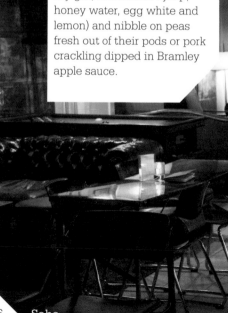

BOB BOB RICARD

1 Upper James Street, W1F 9DF
020 3145 1000,
bobbobricard.com
Mon–Wed 12.30–3pm &
6pm–12am, Thurs 12.30–3pm &
6pm–1am, Fri–Sat 12.30–3pm
& 5.30pm–1am

The 'Press for Champagne' buzzer at each table tells you everything about this dazzling Soho establishment. Russian opulence oozes in the royal blue and gold hued interiors (designed by the late David Collins, famous for the old-style glamour of The Berkeley Hotel's Blue Bar) and in the menu. Here it's British-meets-Russian inspired comfort food, from chicken kiev to beef Wellington. Try the house pale-pink Bloody Mary with a serve of lobster macaroni and cheese, or the Champagne and Truffle Humble Pie. Finish with a strawberries and cream soufflé. Just don't stop pressing that buzzer!

PRESS FOR
CHAMPAGNE

Come to Soho if you're feeling peckish. Have seafood and Champagne at **Randall & Aubin** (14–16 Brewer Street) or modern British at **Refuel** (Soho Hotel, 4 Richmond Mews), **Ducksoup** (41 Dean Street) or **Quo Vadis** (26–29 Dean Street). Spanish delicacies delight at **Barrafina** (54 Frith Street) and **Ember Yard** (60 Berwick Street), Sri Lankan at **Hoppers** (49 Frith Street) and East Coast fare at set-price **Burger & Lobster** (36–38 Dean Street). With kids, head to **Byron Burger** (16–18 Beak Street); for afters, grab a decadent doughnut at **Crosstown Doughnuts** (4 Broadwick Street) or a pretty cake at **Hotel Café Royal** (68 Regent Street). **Blacklock** (basement, 24 Great Windmill Street) is great for charcoal grilled chops and there's also a daily food market on **Berwick Street**.

Experience new theatre writing, cabaret and comedy at the **Soho Theatre** (21 Dean Street, W1D 3NE, sohotheatre.com), where the lively bar is full of creative types enjoying pints and pizza before a show.

The Photographer's Gallery (16–18 Ramillies Street, W1F 7LW, thephotographersgallery.org.uk) is *the* place to see photography – new, old, experimental, daring, sometimes confronting, but always pioneering. There's also a cafe, bookshop and print gallery.

If you're aiming for a West End play or musical on **Shaftesbury Avenue** (or in nearby Covent Garden), book ahead at whatsonstage.com. For last-minute tickets, either try the theatre box office in the morning for possible returns or the **Tkts** (tkts.co.uk) clock-tower booth in **Leicester Square** for seats to some of the best shows.

Ed Burstell has been Managing Director of Liberty London since 2008.

Dean Street Townhouse

(69–71 Dean Street): Part of the members-only Soho House group (but this one's open to the public), it has a chic, cosy atmosphere with delicious British comfort food (they do a killer grilled dover sole) and fun staff.

Liberty London (*see* page 006): OK, so

I'm biased, but I really do shop here, particularly from the Aladdin's cave of the finest collection of rugs and carpets in the world.

Reckless Records (30 Berwick Street): Just one of the many great records shops in Soho (check out too **Sister Ray**, with a vinyl-only store also at the Ace Hotel in Shoreditch, **Sounds of the Universe**, **Harold Moore Music** and **Phonica Records**).

The Box (Walker's Court): For a scandalous outrageous burlesque show that doesn't start until 1am (bookings essential), or for something a little less raunchy, try the **Café de Paris** for a Moulin Rouge style evening. Cocktails essential when seeing cabaret!

Theatreland: I love the **Gielgud**, **Prince of Wales** and **Prince Edward** theatres in Soho (run by the Delfont Mackintosh theatre company) for classy musicals and hit West End plays.

⊕ ANOTHER COUNTRY

➔ **TO MAP RIGHT (VIA CRAWFORD STREET)**

○ PERFUMER H

CRAWFORD STREET

⊕ THE DUKE OF WELLINGTON

PLACE

DORSET STREET

MONTAGU

BRYANSTON MEWS EAST

BRYANSTON

MONTAGU

GLOUCESTER PLACE MEWS

GLOUCESTER

Montagu Square

BRYANSTON

MONTAGU MEWS WEST

MONTAGU

SQUARE

Minotel Wigmore Court London ▪

SQUARE

SQUARE

PLACE

STREET

MONTAGU

GEORGE

GREAT CUMBERLAND PLACE

STREET

The Arch London ▪

Radisson Blu Portman Hotel ▪

SEYMOUR

STREET

BERKELEY

THE GRAZING GOAT

UPPER

The Montcalm ▪

⊕

PLACE

SEYMOUR'S PARLOUR ○

STREET

EDGWARE

SEYMOUR STREET

BRYANSTON

GREAT CUMBERLAND PLACE

MARBLE ARCH

ROAD

Ⓣ

Central line ──

Marble Arch ▪

🚻

MARYLEBONE

There's a unique village feel to Marylebone High Street and its surrounds, with its mix of stylish shopping, delicious eateries and weekend food and vintage markets. It's only just north of Selfridges and St Christopher's Place off Oxford Street, yet feels a long way from the hustle and bustle.

North of Baker Street is **Regent's Park**, one of London's most beautiful royal parks. Don't miss its magnificent gardens with over 12,000 roses (of which there are 400 varieties), the **Open Air Theatre** and at the northern edge, the **ZSL London Zoo**.

24   JUN 8076

ʃHOP
1 **PERFUMER H**
2 **VV ROULEAUX**
3 **DAUNT BOOKS**
4 **MARGARET HOWELL**

17

ʃHOP AND EAT
MOXON ʃTREET
CHILTERN ʃTREET
DRINK
ʃEYMOUR'S PARLOUR

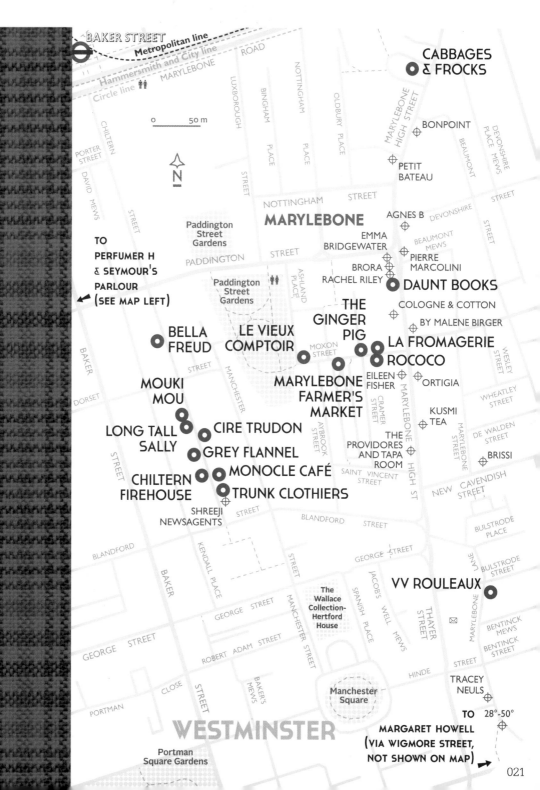

BAKER STREET

Metropolitan line

Hammersmith and City line

Circle line

MARYLEBONE ROAD

NOTTINGHAM ROAD

LUXBOROUGH STREET

BINGHAM PLACE

NOTTINGHAM PLACE

OLDBURY PLACE

MARYLEBONE HIGH STREET

BEAUMONT STREET

DEVONSHIRE PLACE MEWS

CABBAGES & FROCKS

BONPOINT

PETIT BATEAU

PORTER STREET

CHILTERN STREET

DAVID MEWS

STREET

0   50 m

N

NOTTINGHAM STREET

STREET

DEVONSHIRE STREET

AGNES B

MARYLEBONE

Paddington Street Gardens

PADDINGTON STREET

EMMA BRIDGEWATER

BEAUMONT MEWS

PIERRE MARCOLINI

BRORA

RACHEL RILEY

DAUNT BOOKS

TO PERFUMER H & SEYMOUR'S PARLOUR (SEE MAP LEFT)

Paddington Street Gardens

ASHLAND PLACE

THE GINGER PIG

COLOGNE & COTTON

BY MALENE BIRGER

BELLA FREUD

LE VIEUX COMPTOIR

MOXON STREET

LA FROMAGERIE

ROCOCO

BAKER STREET

MANCHESTER STREET

MARYLEBONE FARMER'S MARKET

EILEEN FISHER

CRAMER STREET

ORTIGIA

WESLEY STREET

WHEATLEY STREET

DORSET

MOUKI MOU

AYBROOK STREET

MARYLEBONE HIGH ST

KUSMI TEA

DE WALDEN STREET

MARYLEBONE STREET

LONG TALL SALLY

CIRE TRUDON

GREY FLANNEL

THE PROVIDORES AND TAPA ROOM

BRISSI

STREET

CHILTERN FIREHOUSE

MONOCLE CAFÉ

TRUNK CLOTHIERS

SAINT VINCENT STREET

NEW CAVENDISH STREET

SHREEJI NEWSAGENTS

STREET

BLANDFORD STREET

BULSTRODE PLACE

BLANDFORD

KENDALL PLACE

STREET

GEORGE STREET

JACOBS WELL MEWS

BULSTRODE STREET

BAKER STREET

The Wallace Collection-Hertford House

SPANISH PLACE

VV ROULEAUX

MARYLEBONE LANE

THAYER STREET

BENTINCK MEWS

GEORGE STREET

MANCHESTER STREET

BENTINCK STREET

ROBERT ADAM STREET

STREET

HINDE

TRACEY NEULS

CLOSE

STREET

BAKER'S MEWS

Manchester Square

TO   28°-50°

PORTMAN

WESTMINSTER

MARGARET HOWELL (VIA WIGMORE STREET, NOT SHOWN ON MAP)

Portman Square Gardens

021

1.

PERFUMER H

106A Crawford Street,
W1H 2HZ
020 7258 7859, perfumerh.com
Mon–Sat 10am–6pm

It's very homely in perfumer Lyn Harris's atelier (Britain's only female 'nose'), a ten-minute walk west of Marylebone High Street. It's all gorgeous reclaimed wood, velvet and moody hues. Previously behind Miller Harris, Perfumer H is the next stage in Lyn's olfactory journey. Turning to the UK's flora, foliage and changing seasons for inspiration, new fragrance ideas might incorporate ivy or marmalade, heliotrope or carrot seed. Seasonal fragrances and scented candles reflect the five scent families (citrus, floral, wood, fern and oriental) and Laboratory Editions allows you to buy a fragrance formula outright (your name registered with it in Provence's famed perfume town, Grasse). Everything comes in beautiful bottles and vessels hand-blown by British glassmaker Michael Ruh (personalisation is also available).

VV ROULEAUX

102 Marylebone Lane,
W1U 2QD
020 7224 5179, vvrouleaux.com
Mon–Tues & Fri–Sat
9.30am–6pm, Wed 10.30am–
6pm, Thurs 9.30am–6.30pm

For those with a passion for *passementerie* (decorative trims), you'll never leave VV Rouleaux (rouleaux is French for roll, vv is for very very) empty-handed. Its owner, Annabel Lewis is 'decorating mad', filling the shop with an almost overwhelming cornucopia of ribbons (in every thickness, colour and finish you can imagine, from satin and silk to velvet and vintage-style grosgrain), hand-painted silk flowers (including big blousy English roses), feathers, braiding, pom poms, glittering clips and crystal trims. There are millinery supplies and fancy dress masks too; everything you need to be the belle (or beau) of a ball!

3.

DAUNT BOOKS

83 Marylebone High Street,
W1U 4QW
020 7224 2295,
dauntbooks.co.uk
Mon–Sat 9am–7.30pm,
Sun 11am–6pm

Based in an original
Edwardian bookshop,
Daunt Books is keeping the
magic of bricks-and-mortar
bookstores alive. With its long
oak galleries and graceful
skylights, it feels like walking
into an elegant library rather
than a shop. The staff are
knowledgeable, the selection
of books for adults and
children is enticing, and the
regular book signings and
talks, over a glass of wine,
are always quickly sold out.
They also have branches
in Chelsea, Holland Park,
Cheapside, Hampstead and
Belsize Park.

AMERICA · AFRICA
ASIA · AUSTRALASIA

MARGARET HOWELL

34 Wigmore Street, W1U 2RS
020 7009 9009,
margarethowell.co.uk
Mon–Sat 10am–6pm & Thurs
until 7pm, Sun 12–5pm

Margaret Howell, one of the UK's most respected fashion designers (and most elusive as she rarely gives interviews) specialises in utilitarian understatement, always with a mannish, intelligentsia feel, for both men and women. There is a mix of refinement and roughness in her use of fabrics such as fine gauge knits, slubby linens, Harris tweed, flannel and moleskin, cotton twill and corduroy. Instore, she also celebrates classic British design with iconic furniture pieces by Ercol, Anglepoise lamps and Robert Welch cutlery.

5.

MOXON STREET

Moxon Street is a tiny strip of goodie heaven. Gourmet butcher **The Ginger Pig** (photos 5A and E) does a mean take-away sausage roll or chicken, steak and pork pie; next door **La Fromagerie**'s (photos this page and 5D) shelves and counters overflow with the best quality provisions and magnificent cheeses. It's a perfect spot to meet friends for boiled eggs and coffee in the morning, or the house specialty of Fondue Savoyarde at lunch (on Friday nights, book for the special wine, cheese and charcuterie evenings). A little further along is **Le Vieux Comptoir**, a charcuterie deli and cafe oozing with atmosphere and delicious wines full of French *savoir faire*. Over the road is British chocolate maker Chantal Goad's chocolate emporium **Rococo** (photos 5B, C and F), deftly combining specially sourced cocoa beans with unusual flavours (violet, chilli, raspberry fizz). On Sundays there's the marvellous **Marylebone Farmer's Market** (Cramer Street carpark). Up the road on Saturdays check out **Cabbages & Frocks**, with its mix of new and vintage fashions, crafts and specialty foods, in the grounds of nearby St Marylebone Parish Church.

5A.

5B.

5C.

5D.

5E.

5F.

6.
CHILTERN STREET

Don't miss Chiltern Street, a five-minute walk from the high street. Here the drawcard is the celebrity-favourite restaurant of the **Chiltern Firehouse** hotel (1 Chiltern Street, photo this page), set in a beautifully restored red-bricked Victorian fire station. Star chef Nuno Mendes brings Portuguese, European and Californian flavours to seasonal dishes like smoked burrata or roast heritage carrots, maple-glazed salmon or saddleback pork chops. On a sunny day, it doesn't cost much to sit in the hotel's private courtyard garden with a glass of wine and freshly shucked oysters. For shopping, there are exquisite scented candles by the centuries' old French candlemakers **Cire Trudon** (photo 6A) – they sell Fornasetti's home fragrance collection and a rainbow array of dinner candles – alongside **Monocle Café** (affiliated with the magazine of the same name), elegant, understated menswear at **Trunk Clothiers** (photo 6B) and over the road more fashion and accessories at **Grey Flannel**, **Mouki Mou** and for lean lankies, **Long Tall Sally**. One block north, fashionistas shouldn't miss **Bella Freud**.

7.
SEYMOUR'S PARLOUR
The Zetter Townhouse
28–30 Seymour Street,
W1H 7JB
020 7324 4555,
thezettertownhouse.com
Mon–Wed 7–11am &
12pm–12am, Thurs–Sat 7–11am
& 12pm–1am, Sun 7–11am &
12–11pm

As you sip intriguing concoctions like an Elderberry Kir, Fleur du Mal (Rose & Orris Vodka, lemon and absinthe) or a Two-Pennie Trash (rye whiskey, powdered malts and treacle), whilst sharing one of Seymour's 'Famous Potted Pleasures' (like potted shrimp with nutmeg butter or duck with pomegranate jelly), marvel at the madness of Seymour's Parlour's interiors. Its quirky mix of antique clocks, old school photos, miniature bottles, pieces of architrave and architectural prints on the walls, deep enveloping velvet chairs and a proliferation of (tasteful) 'brown' furniture make this an experience you won't forget in a hurry.

7.

6A.

6B.

7.

Also don't miss on Marylebone High Street: for foodies there's **Kusmi Tea** and chocolatier **Pierre Marcolini**; for fashionistas **By Malene Birger**, **Eileen Fisher**, **Brora** and British cobbler **Tracey Neuls** (29 Marylebone Lane); and for homebods **Brissi, Cologne & Cotton**, and **Emma Bridgewater**. There are lovely scented delights at **Ortigia**, and for kids, there's **Petit Bateau**, **Bonpoint** and royal favourite, **Rachel Riley**. Enjoy a glass of wine and delicious nibbles at **The Providores and Tapa Room** or **28°–50°**, or for a bit of posh pub fare, check out **The Grazing Goat** (6 New Quebec Street).

The Wallace Collection (Hertford House, Manchester Square, W1U 3BN, wallacecollection.org), displayed in the magnificent former home (built in the late 1700s) of a long line of Marquesses of Hertford, houses what's considered to be one of the best collections of paintings, porcelain and furnishings in the UK. There are works by Gainsborough, Velazquez, Ruben and Van Dyck, as well as Sèvres porcelain and Renaissance bronzes. Its French brasserie-style **Wallace Restaurant**, in the light-filled, glass-covered atrium, is a civilised retreat from the outside world, whether for a breakfast omelette or poached Cornish wild sea bass and pommes frites for lunch.

For those with a love for Arthur Conan Doyle's Victorian super sleuth, stop by the eccentric **Sherlock Holmes Museum** (221B Baker Street, NW1 6XE, sherlock-holmes.co.uk). It's all very elementary, my dear reader.

World-renowned perfumer **Lyn Harris** opened her Perfumer H atelier in Marylebone in 2015.

La Fromagerie

(2–6 Moxton Street, *see* page 026): I love Patricia Michelson and her wonderful store which fills me with delight for the seasonal fruits and vegetables, gorgeous meats, selection of breads and the amazing cheese room (I have a passion for Raclette). I love the cafe for lunch with friends.

Shreeji Newsagents

(6 Chiltern Street): The most comprehensive and unusual range of magazines and independent publications, and they'll get anything for you. Amazing service.

Mouki Mou

(29 Chiltern Street): Maria Lemos searches for distinctive and unique designers for her beautiful shop. I love her arts and science shirts and bags, one of the few stockists in Europe.

Monocle Café

(18 Chiltern Street, *see* page 028): For my daily fix of coffee and to read the newspaper. Love the crowd in there too, it always sets me up for the day.

Another Country

(18 Crawford Street): For gifts and beautiful stools and lighting.

Agnes B

(40–41 Marylebone High Street): I love her basic black marcel t-shirts. It always takes me back to living in Paris!

The Duke of Wellington

(94A Crawford Street): Great pub food, atmosphere and a good wine selection.

Fitzrovia is nestled north of Oxford Street up to the Euston Road, west of Regent Street and east to just past Tottenham Court Road. It's mainly offices and apartments but there are lovely shops, eateries and galleries to be found too.

The precinct is watched over by the iconic **BT Tower**, London's tallest building when opened in 1965. Visit the elegant **Fitzroy Square** on the trail of famous residents – look for over a dozen blue plaques on its Georgian and stucco fronted mansions with names such as James McNeill Whistler and George Bernard Shaw. For the young, explore the charming and colourful **Pollock's Toy Museum** (1 Scala Street).

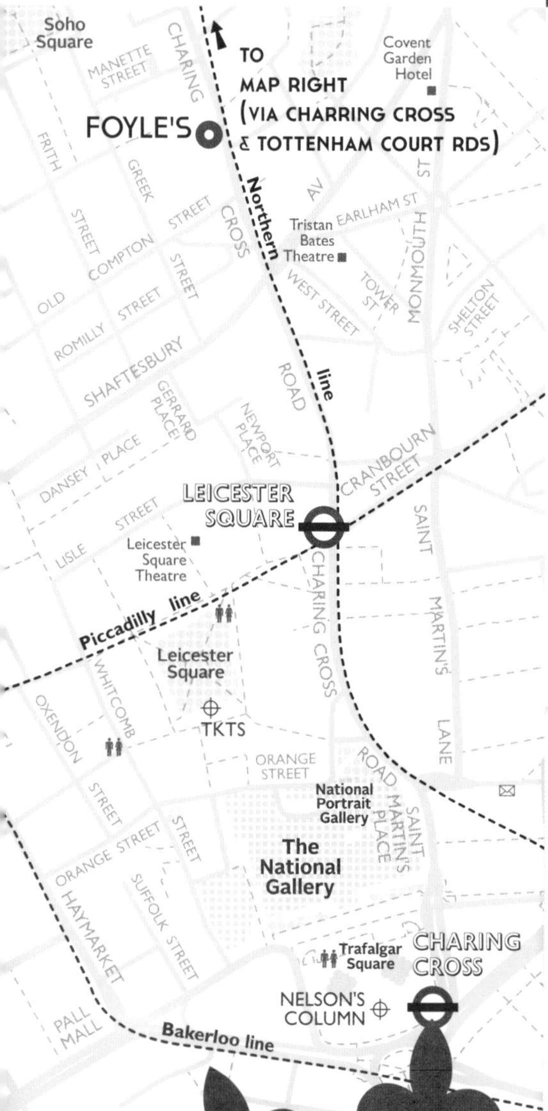
Soho Square
TO MAP RIGHT (VIA CHARRING CROSS & TOTTENHAM COURT RDS)
Covent Garden Hotel
FOYLE'S
Northern line
Tristan Bates Theatre
LEICESTER SQUARE
Leicester Square Theatre
Piccadilly line
Leicester Square
TKTS
National Portrait Gallery
The National Gallery
Trafalgar Square
CHARING CROSS
NELSON'S COLUMN
Bakerloo line

FITZROVIA

SHOP

1 Foyle's
2 Heal's
3 Paperchase

EAT

4 Honey & Co
5 Kaffeine

EAT AND DRINK

6 Berners Tavern
7 The Riding House Cafe

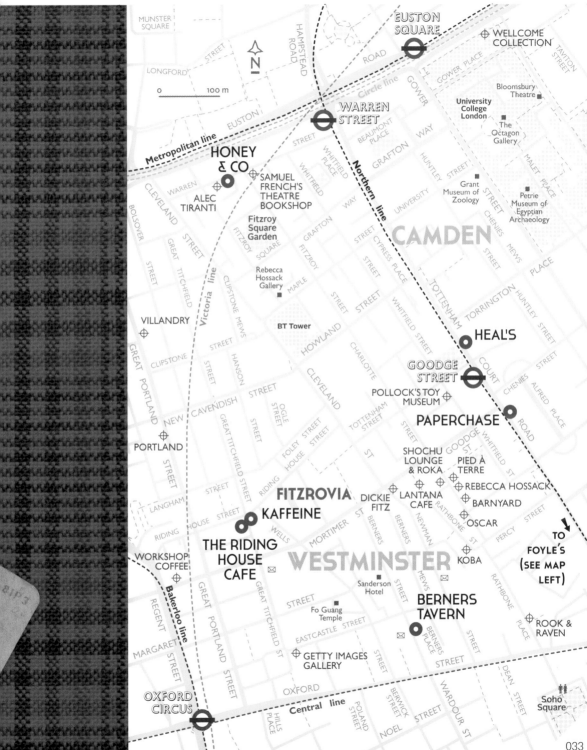

MUNSTER SQUARE

LONGFORD STREET

HAMPSTEAD ROAD

N

0   100 m

EUSTON SQUARE

WELLCOME COLLECTION

Circle line

Metropolitan line

EUSTON

WARREN STREET

GOWER PLACE

GOWER STREET

University College London

Bloomsbury Theatre

The Octagon Gallery

HONEY & CO

SAMUEL FRENCH'S THEATRE BOOKSHOP

ALEC TIRANTI

WARREN STREET

BEAUMONT PLACE

WHITFIELD PLACE

GRAFTON WAY

HUNTLEY STREET

Grant Museum of Zoology

MALET PLACE

Petrie Museum of Egyptian Archaeology

CLEVELAND STREET

BOLSOVER STREET

GREAT TITCHFIELD STREET

Fitzroy Square Garden

Victoria line

FITZROY SQUARE

GRAFTON STREET

FITZROY STREET

Northern line

CYPRESS PLACE

CHENIES STREET

CAMDEN

Rebecca Hossack Gallery

MAPLE STREET

WHITFIELD STREET

TOTTENHAM

TORRINGTON PLACE

HUNTLEY STREET

VILLANDRY

CLIPSTONE MEWS

CLIPSTONE STREET

BT Tower

HOWLAND STREET

CHARLOTTE STREET

HEAL'S

GOODGE STREET

COURT

CHENIES

ALFRED PLACE

HANSON STREET

NEW CAVENDISH STREET

GREAT TITCHFIELD STREET

OGLE STREET

FOLEY STREET

CLEVELAND STREET

TOTTENHAM STREET

POLLOCK'S TOY MUSEUM

PAPERCHASE

GOODGE ST

WHITFIELD ST

ROAD

PORTLAND

NEW CAVENDISH STREET

RIDING HOUSE STREET

SHOCHU LOUNGE & ROKA

PIED À TERRE

REBECCA HOSSACK

LANGHAM STREET

GREAT PORTLAND STREET

RIDING HOUSE STREET

WELLS STREET

FITZROVIA

DICKIE FITZ

LANTANA CAFE

RATHBONE

NEWMAN STREET

BARNYARD

OSCAR

PERCY STREET

RATHBONE PLACE

KAFFEINE

MORTIMER STREET

BERNERS STREET

NEWMAN STREET

KOBA

TO FOYLE'S (SEE MAP LEFT)

WORKSHOP COFFEE

THE RIDING HOUSE CAFE

WESTMINSTER

Sanderson Hotel

Bakerloo line

GREAT PORTLAND STREET

GREAT TITCHFIELD STREET

STREET

Fo Guang Temple

EASTCASTLE STREET

BERNERS STREET

BERNERS PLACE

BERNERS TAVERN

ROOK & RAVEN

MARGARET STREET

REGENT STREET

GETTY IMAGES GALLERY

BERWICK STREET

WARDOUR ST

DEAN STREET

OXFORD CIRCUS

OXFORD STREET

Central line

HILLS PLACE

POLAND STREET

NOEL STREET

Soho Square

1.

FOYLE'S

107 Charing Cross Road,
WC2H 0DT
020 7437 5660, foyles.co.uk
Mon–Sat 9.30am–9pm, Sun
11.30am–6pm

Who said books were
dead? Foyle's set out over a
hundred years ago to be the
best bookshop in the world,
and with its flagship's recent
and impressive revamp, it
quite possibly remains
so. Across five floors, the
shop apparently houses
over 200,000 titles, lots of
signed and special editions,
and the UK's largest foreign
language section, as well
as departments for sheet
music, specialist magazines,
classical and jazz on CD and
vinyl, and a full-schedule
of reader events, from
book signings to children's
storytelling. I've always
thought that if you can't find
what you're looking for at
Foyle's, it doesn't exist.

2.

HEAL'S

196 Tottenham Court Road,
W1T 7LQ
020 7636 1666, heals.co.uk
Mon–Wed & Fri–Sat
10am–7pm, Thurs 10am–8pm,
Sun 12–6pm

Heal's is an iconic British
institution that's borne the
test of time, its heritage
steeped in championing the
Arts and Crafts movement in
furniture and fabric, but today
it's a multi-floored emporium
for the home. Emphasising
the who's who in both British
and international design, old
and new, means you'll find
Eames chairs and William
Morris rugs alongside
Cressida Bell trays and Lee
Broom crystal light bulbs. The
make-your-own neon wall
lighting is affordable and
fun, and easily transportable
too. Ascend the original Cecil
Brewer staircase to see great
design in action at the **Forge
& Co** all-day brasserie, filled
with furniture pieces on sale,
alongside dishes like eggs
benedict, steak tartare or a
classic Eton mess.

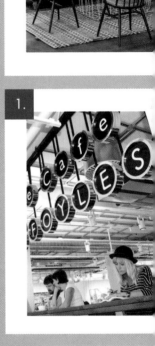

3.

PAPERCHASE

213–215 Tottenham Court Road, W1T 7PS
020 7467 6200,
paperchase.co.uk
Mon–Wed & Fri 8.30am–7.30pm, Thurs 8.30am–8pm, Sat 9am–7pm, Sun 11.30am–6pm

---

It doesn't matter if you're ten or 100 years old, it's hard to resist the technicoloured paraphernalia on sale in this enormous stationery store (Paperchase also has many offshoots around the city). Packed to the brim with all your paper needs, it's fun, funky and often quite seriously kitsch. The ground floor is dedicated to cards and gift-wrapping, and its own in-house-designed collections of notebooks, folders, pens and lunchboxes that change in theme each season so there's always something new to tempt you. There's a vast section of leather and desk accessories and magazines on the first floor (along with a cafe that makes good coffee, cakes and sandwiches) and on the second floor, a space dedicated to art papers and craft supplies.

001   011   240   010

.020   030   050   060

070   080   090   081

051   120   110   101

4.

HONEY & CO

25A Warren Street, W1T 5LZ
020 7388 6175,
honeyandco.co.uk
Mon–Fri 8am–10.30pm,
Sat 9.30am–10.30pm

Never has a more
unspectacular, cramped
restaurant caused so much
excitement with London
foodies. Run by Israeli
husband-and-wife team
Itamar Srulovich and Sarit
Packer (both Ottolenghi
alumni), they have two award-
winning cookbooks under
their belt, inspired by the food
from their childhoods growing
up in Israel. The kitchen here
is like an extension of their
home, the space filled with
the scent of aromatic spices.
Try the glorious Fitzrovia
buns (their take on the
iconic Chelsea currant and
butter swirl) or baked egg
and tomato Shakshuka for
breakfast, the slow-cooked
chicken with pomegranate
Musakhan for dinner and the
strawberry semolina spliffs for
dessert. Food just like their
mothers and aunties used
to make.

5.

KAFFEINE

66 Great Titchfield Street,
W1W 7QJ
020 7580 6755, kaffeine.co.uk
Mon–Fri 7.30am–6pm, Sat
8.30am–6pm, Sun 9am–5pm

- -

A coffee-obsessed friend of mine won't go anywhere else but here for her fix of rich, strong espresso (and the fact the staff greet customers by name, an unusual touch for a big city like London). Small and compact, it has a buzzy vibe and a community feel, brimming with regulars who come for the Aussie-style coffee and delicious breakfast and lunchtime staples, made almost entirely from scratch, including 'French retro' baguettes, stuffed focaccia, tarts and simple salads. All inspired by what's best in season.

6.

BERNERS TAVERN

The London Edition Hotel,
10 Berners Street, W1T 3NP
020 7908 7979,
bernerstavern.com
Mon–Fri 7–10.30am, 12–3pm,
3.30–4.30pm & 5pm–12am,
Sat 9am–4pm & 5pm–12am,
Sun 9am–4pm & 6pm–12am

With its double-height ceilings and restored Edwardian plaster work walls, covered with over 300 gilt-framed paintings and pictures, Berners Tavern, located in Ian Schrager's Edition hotel, is a feast of grandeur. With grand chandeliers and plush velvet booths, the seasonal British menu overseen by hot Brit chef Jason Atherton takes you from breakfast (full English with black pudding or healthy steel-cut porridge) to dinner (updated classics like lobster chopped salad or truffled beef Wellington). For weekend brunch there's slow-cooked Romney Marsh lamb and flaming Alaska. Head to the Punch Room (bookings essential) for an intimate, unique experience of specialty punches, crafted to order, served in antique tureens with crystal glasses.

7.

THE RIDING HOUSE CAFE

43–51 Great Titchfield Street,
W1W 7PQ
020 7927 0840,
ridinghousecafe.co.uk
Mon–Thurs 7.30am–11.30pm,
Fri 7.30am–12.30am, Sat 9am–
12.30am, Sun 9am–10.30pm

The Riding House Cafe was one of the first to corner the salvaged industrial chic aesthetic, now much imitated throughout the city. With an emphasis on light, healthy loveliness, this brasserie serves up good-for-you superfood salads and fresh blitzed juices, perfect for a green fix when you're travelling, but it's not all puritanical either – beef and bone marrow burgers and Chinese chicken wings (with a hint of lavender) are on the menu too. You can come and go as you please, as dressed up or down as you like, with a communal table for those flying solo, low-lying chairs in which to sip cocktails, and nooks and crannies to share gossip over a Cucumber Mary Jane and a bowl of maple-glazed root vegetables.

7.

6.

7.

6.

Fitzrovia boasts a huge variety of top-notch foodie spots to suit every tastebud. Along Great Portland Street, enjoy lunch at **Portland** or try the fresh salad, sweet and savoury bar at **Villandry**. On Newman Street, try Antipodean-fused all-day brasserie fare at **Dickie Fitz**. Charlotte Street owes its creative vibe to the mix of galleries and global cuisine – from Japanese at **Roka** to rustic, finger-lickin' good nosh at **Barnyard**, French at **Pied à Terre** and Korean barbecue at **Koba** (11 Rathbone Street). Enjoy tempura seaweed with a Twisted Mojito, muddled with passionfruit puree, at **Charlotte Street Hotel's** bar **Oscar** whilst admiring its Bloomsbury-inspired mural by artist Alex Hollweg.

For keen model makers and sculptors, don't miss arts and crafts supplier **Alec Tiranti** (27 Warren Street), for drama queens (and kings) visit **The Samuel French Theatre Bookshop** (52 Fitzroy Street).

The **Wellcome Collection** (183 Euston Road, NW1 2BE, wellcomecollection.org) celebrates an extraordinary collection of over two million objects and books amassed by the pioneering pharmacist Sir Henry Wellcome. Exhibitions, talks, a research library and cafe prove the perfect environment for visitors to ponder the importance and magic of medicine past, present and future.

Admire (and buy, if budget allows) iconic 20th century photography by Slim Aarons and Patrick Lichfield at **Getty Images Gallery** (46 Eastcastle Street, W1W 8DX, gettyimagesgallery.com). For original and editioned artworks by innovative, young artists visit **Rook & Raven** (7 Rathbone Place, W1T 1HN, rookandraven.co.uk).

Pia Benham is head of textiles, upholstery and own-label collections at Heal's.

Rebecca Hossack (28 Charlotte Street): A wonderful art gallery always full of lovely pieces, from little things to take away to big pieces of statement art, from emerging artists to big name stars. Run by charismatic Aussie owner Rebecca Hossack (responsible for championing Australian Indigenous art in the UK when she first opened in 1988). Worth a visit.

Lantana Cafe (13 Charlotte Place): Great selection of food for a quick lunch, clean scrubbed tables, nice atmosphere and friendly staff.

Workshop Coffee (80A Mortimer Street): A friendly coffee shop with a local vibe, the perfect place to grab a coffee en route to work or the shops.

The Riding House Cafe (*see* page 040): A great place to meet for an early morning breakfast, full of charm. They do a great menu. My particular favourite is the eggs benedict.

Shochu Lounge (37 Charlotte Street): Downstairs at Japanese restaurant Roka, famous for its robata grill, this is a real treat, a fun place to spend an evening, always busy and vibrant when needing a change of scenery or a cocktail!

East of Tottenham Court Road lies Bloomsbury, best known as home to the famed Bloomsbury group of writers and artists like Virginia Woolf and Lytton Strachey who lived here in the early 20th century. It's also where you'll find the awe-inspiring British Museum (*see page 052*).

Grab a coffee from the cafe in Russell Square's public garden and sit, enjoying the blossom and birdsong. Pop into the quirky **Cartoon Museum** (35 Little Russell Street) or step back in time at **James Smith & Sons** (53 New Oxford Street) for 180 years' worth of umbrella and cane-making history.

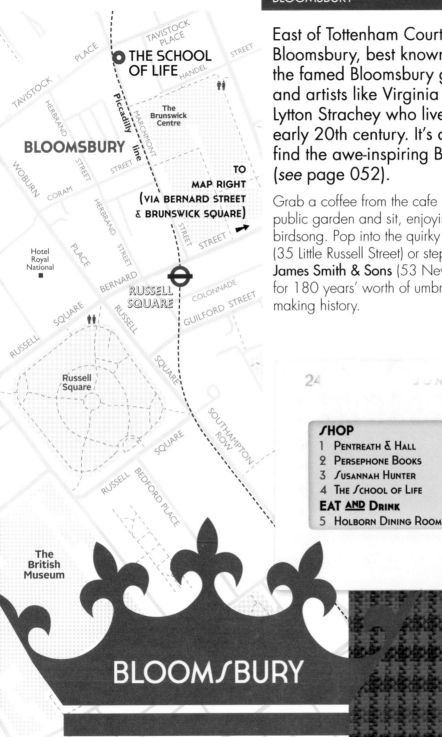

24   JUN 8016

ƒHOP
1 PENTREATH & HALL
2 PERSEPHONE BOOKS
3 ƒUSANNAH HUNTER
4 THE ƒCHOOL OF LIFE

EAT AND DRINK
5 HOLBORN DINING ROOM

BLOOMƒBURY

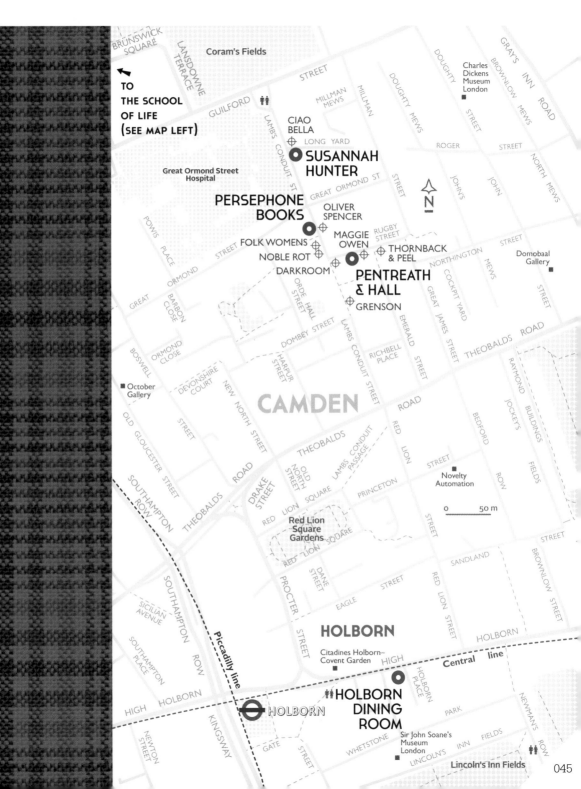

TO
THE SCHOOL
OF LIFE
(SEE MAP LEFT)

Coram's Fields

BRUNSWICK SQUARE

LANSDOWNE TERRACE

GUILFORD STREET

STREET

MILLMAN MEWS

MILLMAN

DOUGHTY MEWS

DOUGHTY STREET

BROWNLOW MEWS

GRAY'S INN ROAD

Charles
Dickens
Museum
London

LAMBS CONDUIT ST

CIAO
BELLA

LONG YARD

● SUSANNAH
HUNTER

GREAT ORMOND ST

ROGER STREET

STREET

JOHN'S STREET

JOHN STREET

NORTH MEWS

Great Ormond Street
Hospital

PERSEPHONE
BOOKS

OLIVER
SPENCER

MAGGIE
OWEN

RUGBY STREET

N

POWIS PLACE

STREET

FOLK WOMENS

NOBLE ROT

DARKROOM

THORNBACK
& PEEL

NORTHINGTON STREET

COCKPIT YARD

STREET

Domobaal
Gallery

GREAT ORMOND

BARBON CLOSE

ORDE HALL STREET

● PENTREATH
& HALL

GRENSON

EMERALD STREET

GREAT JAMES STREET

MEWS

THEOBALDS ROAD

RAYMOND BUILDINGS

STREET

ORMOND CLOSE

DOMBEY STREET

HARPUR STREET

LAMBS CONDUIT STREET

RICHBELL PLACE

RAYMOND BUILDINGS

BOSWELL STREET

DEVONSHIRE COURT

NEW NORTH STREET

CAMDEN

ROAD

RED LION

JOCKEY'S FIELDS

■ October
Gallery

OLD GLOUCESTER STREET

STREET

THEOBALDS

OLD NORTH STREET

THEOBALDS

LAMBS CONDUIT PASSAGE

RED LION

STREET

■ Novelty
Automation

BEDFORD ROW

DRAKE STREET

SQUARE

PRINCETON STREET

0   50 m

SICILIAN AVENUE

SOUTHAMPTON ROW

Piccadilly line

PROCTER STREET

RED LION

Red Lion
Square
Gardens

SQUARE

RED LION

STREET

SANDLAND STREET

BROWNLOW STREET

SOUTHAMPTON PLACE

SOUTHAMPTON ROW

DANE STREET

EAGLE STREET

RED LION STREET

HOLBORN

Citadines Holborn–
Covent Garden

HIGH

Central line

HOLBORN

HIGH HOLBORN

HOLBORN PLACE

HOLBORN

● HOLBORN
DINING
ROOM

NEWMAN'S ROW

KINGSWAY

NEWTON STREET

GATE STREET

WHETSTONE

Sir John Soane's
Museum
London

PARK

LINCOLN'S INN

FIELDS

Lincoln's Inn Fields

1.

PENTREATH & HALL
17 Rugby Street, WC1N 3QT
020 7430 2526,
pentreath-hall.com
Mon—Sat 11am—6pm

There is an old-style elegance
mixed with a crazy curiosity
shop feel to the 'goods and
furnishings' on display at
Pentreath & Hall, run by
architect and blogger Ben
Pentreath and decorative
artist and maker Bridie Hall.
Bright and colourful, there
seems no rhyme or reason
(but a lot of fun and beauty)
to the array of pieces for sale.
From geometric cushions and
prints by 20th century artists
Eric Ravilious and Edward
Bawden or block-printed
originals of the English
countryside by Howard
Phipps, to pretty engraved
glasses with butterflies and
Astier de Villatte geometric-
printed plates, Hall's own
Camellia decoupage trays,
plaster casts of lion's heads
and brightly coloured turned
resin lampbases. There are
even antique Staffordshire
spongeware spaniels.

2.
PERSEPHONE BOOKS
59 Lamb's Conduit Street,
WC1N 3NB
020 7242 9292,
persephonebooks.co.uk
Mon–Fri 10am–6pm,
Sat 12–5pm

Publishing reprints of long-forgotten fiction and non-fiction was a daring initiative when Nicola Beauman launched Persephone Books in 1999. She's since gone on to publish over 100 books, mainly by mid 20th century female writers on everything from memoirs and short stories to cookery books (with modern prefaces written by major authors like Jilly Cooper, Diana Athill and Julian Barnes). There's something immediately pleasing about the way they've given each book a simple grey cover and a vintage fabric-inspired endpaper and matching bookmark.

3.
SUSANNAH HUNTER
84 Lamb's Conduit Street,
WC1N 3LR
020 7692 3798,
susannahhunter.com
Mon–Fri 10am–6pm,
Sat 11am–5pm

There aren't too many handbag designers who can say they've won Silver at the Chelsea Flower Show, but Susannah's exquisitely vibrant, dramatic appliquéd leather blooms on handbags and purses, footstools and folding screens are worthy (she created a 'garden' of floral-festooned panels and plants inspired by Massachusetts). Susannah combines her passion for art and fashion to create these little works of art – each piece, whether a tote bag or iPad cover, is hand-cut and stitched from drawings of her favourite flowers, such as roses, foxgloves, poppies, passion flowers and anemones. 'Graphic shapes yet with a delicate beauty about them,' she says.

4.

THE SCHOOL OF LIFE

70 Marchmont Street,
WC1N 1AB
020 7833 1010,
theschooloflife.com
Mon–Sat 10am–6pm

If your travels are requiring
a little soul searching, it
might pay to pop into The
School of Life – a happy,
uplifting place devoted
to developing emotional
intelligence through
cultural understanding and
pursuits. There are courses
on everything from how
to get a good night's sleep
to dealing with conflict
and procrastinating less.
But if that's all a little too
seriously heady for you,
just go shopping instead:
there are Conversation
Placemats of Interesting
Guests, philosophical honey
(from the birthplaces of
three great Greek thinkers),
witty key tags (perfectionist,
philosophical, idiosyncratic)
and box sets of 'how to'
guides (stay sane, think
more about sex, thrive in the
digital age, etc.) for changing
your life.

5.

HOLBORN DINING ROOM

252 High Holborn, WC1V 7EN
020 3747 8633,
holborndiningroom.com
Mon–Fri 7am–11.30pm,
Sat 8am–11.30pm, Sun
8am–10.30pm

Holborn is a bit of a funny
old no-man's land and a busy
thoroughfare that dates back
to Roman times, but the
glamorous Rosewood Hotel
in all its marbled, Cuban
mahogany and gilded glass
splendour makes it worth
visiting. Inside, the Holborn
Dining Room feels warm and
welcoming with materials
like reclaimed wood, red
leather, tweed and antique
copper-topped bars, and
it's one of the only places in
London where you can get
a proper Sunday breakfast
before lunchtime. Rest weary
feet whilst enjoying an Isle of
Wight tomato salad or award-
winning Scotch egg, dressed
Cornish crab or luxurious
burger (or take-away a
roast beef and horseradish
mayo sandwich and an
Eccles cake).

GOOD IDEAS FOR EVERYDAY LIFE

70

LOSE YOUR DREAMS
— And You Will —
LOSE YOUR MIND

THE SCHOOL OF LIFE

OPEN

SHOP
CLASSES
WEEKENDS
TALKS
THERAPY

While mooching around Lamb's Conduit Street – a charming pedestrianised strip of shops and cafes with a distinctly British feel – find handsome, handmade shoes at **Grenson**, well-priced modern menswear with the quality of tailoring at **Oliver Spencer**, and graphic installation-style designs by rising stars at **Darkroom**. Off Rugby Street, **Thornback & Peel's** homeware textile prints offer a quirky, modern take on nostalgic wood engravings.

You could spend days at the **British Museum** (Great Russell Street, WC1B 3DG, britishmuseum.org) and still not see all of its extraordinary collection of artefacts, from 3rd century Chinese ceramics to ancient Egyptian tomb art and evolutionary remnants from 2000BC Mesopotamia. Within its original 19th century architectural surrounds, its soaring domed ceiling and contemporary Norman Foster designed Great Court, it's a wonderful place to learn about history in vivid, glorious detail.

Nearby, at **Sir John Soane's Museum** (13 Lincoln's Inn Fields, WC2A 3BP, soane.org), the famous Victorian architect (responsible for the Bank of England) amassed a treasure trove of 'loot', from antiquities and curiosities to sculptures, furniture and paintings by the likes of Hogarth and Turner. All are still on display in what was his former home, as he left it when he died; you never know what you'll see or learn.

Handbag designer **Susannah Hunter** has lived and worked in Bloomsbury for 15 years.

Ciao Bella (86–90 Lamb's Conduit Street): The friendliest, most welcoming local Italian restaurant in the world. Spaghetti Pomodoro and a glass of Falanghina Villa Mathilde anytime.

Maggie Owen (13 Rugby Street): A gorgeous treasure trove of amazing, unique jewellery and accessories.

Folk Womens (53 Lamb's Conduit Street): Essential stop-off for my seasonal fix of Folk Shoes and Belgian label Humanoid, among other things.

L. Cornelissen & Son (105 Great Russell Street): Fabulous art materials. I've been in awe of the wonderful colourful pigments there since I was a student at Central Saint Martins.

Noble Rot (51 Lamb's Conduit Street): A new addition to the area, opened by the duo behind wine specialist magazine *Noble Rot*. It's fast become my favourite place for an after-work drink and a delicious oyster or two.

COVENT GARDEN

Famous as a bustling fruit, veg and flower market in the 1800s, Covent Garden's cobble-stoned piazza still lies at the heart of the precinct's retail trade. Nearby are some of London's greatest galleries and squares, including the famous Trafalgar Square, giving you no shortage of sights to see.

Enjoy the piazza's daily **Apple**, **Jubilee** and **East Colonnade** markets, with stalls touting everything from antique bottles to old printing blocks. Long Acre has high street brands galore; Neal, Henrietta and James streets and Seven Dials feature independent boutiques and cafes; St Martin's Lane boasts a busy theatre strip, and there's a plethora of men's urbanwear stores on Earlham Street.

24   JUN 8016

SHOP
1 ARAM
2 BROMPTON JUNCTION
3 CHARLOTTE TILBURY
  BEAUTY BOUDOIR
4 ORLA KIELY
5 LAWRENCE ALKIN GALLERY
6 STANFORDS
7 STEPHEN JONES

17

EAT
THE IVY
FERNANDEZ & WELLS
SALON AT SPRING

HOLBORN

Central line

OXFORD STREET

N

LAWRENCE
ALKIN
GALLERY

CAMDEN

STEPHEN
JONES

Piccadilly line

New London Theatre

0   50 m

BROMPTON
JUNCTION

Seven Dials Hotel

COVENT
GARDEN

MONMOUTH
COFFEE

Radisson Blu Edwardian

ORLA KIELY

CAUDALIE

DONMAR
WAREHOUSE

Cambridge Theatre

COVENT
GARDEN

Royal
Opera
House

AUGUSTUS
HARRIS

TATTY
DEVINE

THE
IVY

LES NÉRÉIDES

CHARLOTTE
TILBURY
BEAUTY
BOUDOIR

London
Film
Museum

THE
TINTIN
SHOP

AGNES B

STANFORDS

London
Transport
Museum

THE LAMB
& FLAG

THE IVY
MARKET
GRILL

St Pauls
Church

LAIRD
LONDON

LEICESTER
SQUARE

WESTMINSTER

Adelphi
Theatre

TO
FERNANDEZ
& WELLS, ARAM &
SALON AT SPRING
(SEE MAP LEFT)

English
National Opera
(ENO)

Northern line

WILLIAM IV STREET

ARAM

110 Drury Lane, WC2B 5SG
020 7557 7557, aram.co.uk
Mon–Wed & Fri–Sat 10am–
6pm, Thurs 10am–7pm

For the past 50 years, Aram
has been bringing innovative
modern design to London –
from Marcel Breuer and
Scarpa to Le Corbusier
and Charlotte Perriand –
and establishing special
relationships with the likes of
Eileen Gray to reproduce and
distribute her work. While you
might not take home one of
Gray's Bibendum armchairs,
perhaps one of the following
would fit nicely into your
suitcase: a Barber Osgerby
Olio jug, Alexander Girard for
Vitra wooden doll, Chisel &
Mouse's handmade miniature
plaster replica of the Battersea
Power Station or Nick Munro
for Aram's Fasto stainless
steel cocktail shaker (inspired
by the instruments and
music at the infamous Ronnie
Scott's jazz club nearby).

2.

BROMPTON JUNCTION
76 Long Acre, WC2E 9JS
020 7836 5700, brompton.com
Mon–Fri 9am–7pm, Sat
10am–6pm, Sun 12–5pm

As a bike is now *de rigeur* in the city thanks to the introduction of the 'Boris bike' in 2010 (the free-bicycle scheme where anyone can hire a bike to get around the city, initiated by former Mayor Boris Johnson), the Brompton foldable is the city commuter's bicycle of choice. Invented by Andrew Ritchie in 1975, over 45,000 of these bikes are made per year, each hand-brazed by skilled craftspeople at their London factory to exact customer specifications. At the flagship Brompton Junction store (on the same site that saw the invention of the hobby horse bicycle in 1819) there's a cafe, selection of spare parts and accessories, demonstration bikes to test drive, and touch-screen technology to help you custom build your own bike. And of course, rows and rows of brightly coloured Bromptons.

3.

CHARLOTTE TILBURY BEAUTY BOUDOIR
11–12 James Street, WC2E 8BT
020 3846 9469,
charlottetilbury.com
Mon–Sat 10am–9pm,
Sun 10.30am–6pm

To know the secrets behind what makes the A-listers shine so bright, head for a lesson at celebrity make-up artist Charlotte Tilbury's flagship store. Kate Moss, Demi Moore, Penelope Cruz and Keira Knightley are just a few of the rollcall of beauties she's worked with. Upstairs, peruse Charlotte's best selling lippies, make-up kits and cosmetic bags (which make perfect gifts); downstairs, the scene is dazzling – Art Deco mirrored dressing tables, a red velvet buttoned conversation settee and rock'n'roll flourishes of ostrich feathers and palm frond chandeliers. Learn how to achieve a signature Charlotte Tilbury look, from 'Vintage Vamp' to 'Glamour Muse' and 'Bombshell', with a drop-in tutorial by one of her team.

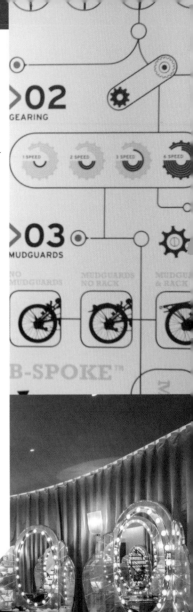

4.

ORLA KIELY

31 Monmouth Street,
WC2H 9DD
020 7240 4022, orlakiely.com
Mon–Sat 10am–6.30pm,
Sun 12–5pm

Irish designer Orla Kiely
translates her keen eye for
a mid-century-inspired
aesthetic and retro colour
palette into the motifs,
clothing and furniture
designs for each season's
collection of fashion, beauty
and homewares. Her designs
have gone international
but here, in her flagship
store, Orla's bold, geometric
designs of flowers, owls, cars,
boats, pears and tulips – and
most notably her signature
stem print – can be found
embossed or printed on bags
or woven into towels. A great
spot for picking up presents.

5.

LAWRENCE ALKIN GALLERY

42 New Compton Street,
WC2H 8DA
020 7240 7909,
lawrencealkingallery.com
Mon–Sat 11am–7pm

You just might pick up a
Banksy at the Lawrence
Alkin Gallery if you're very,
very lucky. Specialising in
contemporary, urban, street
and pop art, Lawrence aims
to foster emerging talent
and bring iconic works to
the public at (relatively)
affordable prices through
limited edition prints at the
gallery. There are works by
Jessica Albarn (Damon's
sister), graffitist Ben Ein,
punk artist Jamie Reid
and photography by Mario
Testino; and even a few
prints by Andy Warhol and
Peter Blake.

KEATON HENSON

6.

STANFORDS
12–14 Long Acre, WC2E 9LP
020 7836 1321, stanfords.co.uk
Mon–Sat 9am–8pm,
Sun 11.30am–6pm

Stanfords isn't just a travel bookshop – it's *the* place to go for finding all sorts of ways to navigate every nook and cranny of the world. Opened in 1901, it's the largest stockist of maps (walking, driving, cycling) and travel books (from guide books to travel memoirs) in the world; a favourite source of information and inspiration for famous adventurers including Ernest Shackleton, Florence Nightingale, Ranulph Fiennes and Michael Palin. There's practical travel kit too – adaptors and chargers, first aid kits and mosquito nets, even a reproduction of a brass compass from the 19th century campaign trail. You might need a compass to navigate the shop, spread over three floors.

7.

STEPHEN JONES
36 Great Queen Street,
WC2B 5AA
020 7242 0770,
stephenjonesmillinery.com
Mon–Wed & Fri 10am–6pm,
Thurs 11am–7pm

Not only is Stephen Jones the fashion world's favourite milliner, alongside Philip Treacy of course, but he's also one of the nicest men you could possibly meet. Stephen's millinery career extends from the days of being a Blitz nightclub kid to working with the likes of Dior (with both John Galliano and Raf Simons), Vivienne Westwood, Louis Vuitton, the Metropolitan Museum of Art and Jasper Conran. Here in his atelier, feel like a rock star or royalty (all of whom are customers) by picking up a jaunty little beret or trilby from his Miss Jones or Jonesboy collections. Or if you're feeling flush, commission a couture creation.

8.

THE IVY

1–5 West Street, WC2H 9NQ
020 7836 4751, the-ivy.co.uk
Mon–Wed 12–11.30pm,
Thurs–Sat 12pm–12am,
Sun 12–10.30pm

Anyone who is/was/will be anyone wouldn't miss The Ivy – one night I saw Cilla Black, Lionel Ritchie, Julia Ormond, Hugh Grant and Claudia Schiffer, all at different tables. When it closed for renovation it was much missed on the London restaurant scene. Now it's back, prettier and buzzier than ever, still with its much-admired stained-glass harlequin windows and comforting dark wood panelling. But whilst not as impossible to get into as it once was, book ahead to avoid a wait. If you're turning up on the off chance, it's fun to pull up a seat at the central bar, order a crispy duck salad with watermelon and cashews or the roast Devonshire chicken with pommes sarladaise between two, teamed with a chamomile-infused Bees Knees gin cocktail, and people watch. The Ivy has sister restaurants in Chelsea, Kensington, Marylebone and another in Covent Garden (Henrietta Street).

9.

FERNANDEZ & WELLS

Somerset House, Strand,
WC2R 1LA
020 7420 9408,
fernandezandwells.com
Mon–Fri 8am–10pm, Sat
10am–10pm, Sun 10am–8pm

- -

Fernandez & Wells founders
Jorge Fernandez and Rick
Wells first set up in Soho's
Lexington Street and then
Beak Street, transforming the
area's cafe culture with great
coffee, delectable homemade
cakes and a simple selection
of delicious toasted paninis.
It was uncomplicated and
understated but it worked.
The Somerset House branch
is one of my favourites,
enhanced by the light
and airiness that comes
with the double-height
windows and ceilings of
the building's neoclassical
design. It's the perfect spot
to stop after touring one
of Somerset House's great
exhibitions and there's also a
fantastic **Rizzoli** bookshop
next door.

10

SALON AT SPRING

Somerset House, Lancaster Place,
WC2R 1LA
020 3011 0115,
springrestaurant.co.uk
Mon–Sat 12–11pm, Sun 12–5pm

If you don't fancy a big blow-out lunch but still want to treat the tastebuds to something unique, head to Salon, within the inner sanctum of Skye Gyngell's Spring restaurant at Somerset House. Australian-born Skye made her name as head chef at Petersham Nurseries in Richmond, where her 'fork to fork' mentality (much of the produce used was grown in the nursery's kitchen garden) is still very much at play here as Skye now works with British biodynamic fruit and vegetable growers Fern Varrow. Salon is relaxed and informal, the perfect place, with a Moscato Spritz (laced with Campari) in hand, to experience the wonder of Skye's elegant seasonal cuisine.

Covent Garden has excellent specialty shopping including French skincare at **Caudalie** (39 Monmouth Street), comics and gifts at **The Tintin Shop** (34 Floral Street), and gentleman's hipster hats at **Laird London** (23 New Row). For a good ale and ploughman's, visit Dickens' favourite pub **The Lamb & Flag** (33 Rose Street).

Smoked salmon sandwiches and a glass of bubbles in the majestic glass-domed Floral Hall of the **Royal Opera House** (Bow Street, WC2E 9DD, roh.org.uk) is a must before a performance by either the Royal Opera or Ballet companies (advance bookings recommended).

Journey from horse-drawn cab to the development of the city's centuries' old Underground system at the **London Transport Museum** (Covent Garden Piazza, WC2E 7BB, ltmuseum.co.uk).

Head to the neoclassical **Somerset House** (Strand, WC2R 1LA, somersethouse.org.uk) for fashion and photography exhibitions, design fairs, music gigs and film-screenings.

Trafalgar Square, a city landmark since the 13th century, is where tourists and pigeons alike meet at the base of **Nelson's column** (gallantly guarded by four monumental bronze lions). At **The National Gallery** (Trafalgar Square, WC2N 5DN, nationalgallery.org.uk) find Vermeer and Rubens, Gainsborough and Van Gogh; at **The National Portrait Gallery** (NPG, St Martin's Place, WC2H 0HE, npg.org.uk), view portraits of Kate Moss to Bowie, King Henry VIII to the Duchess of Cambridge. Its top floor **Portrait Restaurant** has fantastic views down Whitehall to the Houses of Parliament and Big Ben.

Ruth Aram is head of retail at Aram.

Somerset House (*see* opposite page): With its grand proportions, it's an oasis of calm. Alfresco eating in summer, ice-skating in winter and interesting exhibitions all year round.

Tatty Devine (44 Monmouth Street): I love their bright witty designs – they always have a great selection of brooches which inject a bit of humour and colour into my rather austere work wardrobe.

Monmouth Coffee (27 Monmouth Street): A real institution for coffee lovers, there's usually a queue waiting patiently outside but it moves quickly. My eldest daughter Izzy loves to sit with me in the upstairs booths because the place is unique and unlike the run-of-the-mill chains.

Augustus Harris (33 Catherine Street): A newly opened Venetian-style *bacaro*, with a limited menu of delicious crostini, cheeses and salamis, excellent cocktails and friendly staff. It's already a firm favourite with the staff of Aram.

Agnes B (35–36 Floral Street): After 20 years, still the designer I rely on for well made, stylish separates that are comfortable and confidence boosting.

Donmar Warehouse (41 Earlham Street): This tiny theatre has a devoted following who often book ahead without knowing what they are going to see. The front rows are inches from the stage ensuring an immersive experience.

King's Cross has gentrified beyond its past as one of London's seedier red light districts to become far more than just the place to catch the Eurostar. Thanks to a multi-billion-pound regeneration of both King's Cross and St Pancras stations, and development of the surrounding 67 acres of land and canal ways, there's so much to see and eat.

The former warehouses and dock areas have been transformed into a thriving restaurant scene. There are public parks created in former gas holders, gardens planted in skips, and even a self-cleaning natural swimming pond (complete with wood-fired sauna) to swim in. And for *Harry Potter* buffs, don't miss Platform 9¾.

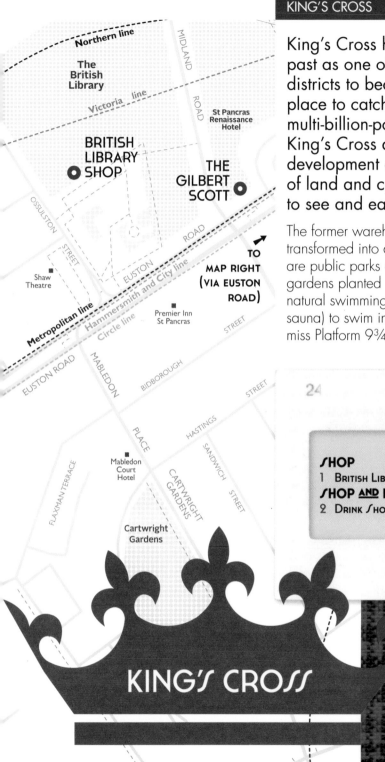

Northern line

The British Library

Victoria line

MIDLAND ROAD

St Pancras Renaissance Hotel

BRITISH LIBRARY SHOP

THE GILBERT SCOTT

OSSULSTON STREET

Shaw Theatre

Metropolitan line

Hammersmith and City line

Circle line

EUSTON ROAD

Premier Inn St Pancras

TO MAP RIGHT (VIA EUSTON ROAD)

STREET

EUSTON ROAD

MABLEDON PLACE

BIDBOROUGH STREET

HASTINGS STREET

SANDWICH STREET

FLAXMAN TERRACE

Mabledon Court Hotel

CARTWRIGHT GARDENS

Cartwright Gardens

KING'S CROSS

24   JUN 2016

SHOP
1   BRITISH LIBRARY SHOP
SHOP **AND** EAT
2   DRINK SHOP DO

17

EAT
GRAIN STORE
GRANGER & CO
EAT **AND** DRINK
DISHOOM
THE GILBERT SCOTT

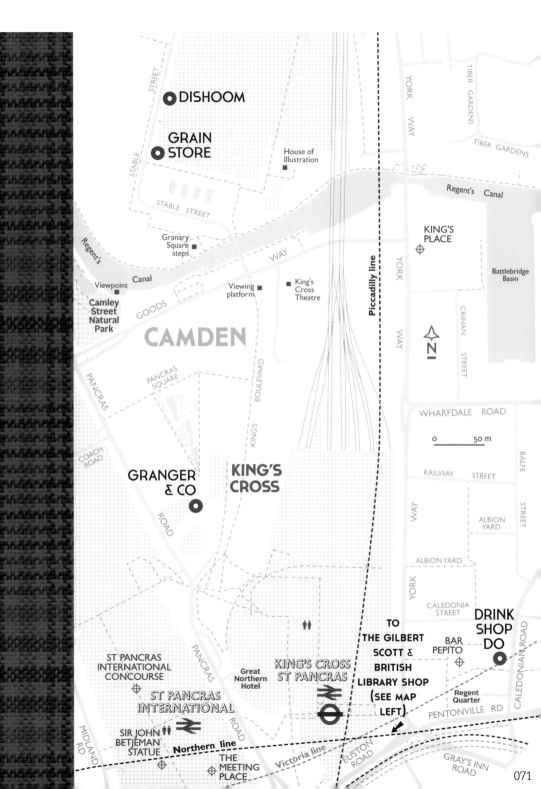

DISHOOM

GRAIN
STORE

House of
Illustration

STABLE STREET

STABLE STREET

KING'S
PLACE

Regent's Canal

Battlebridge
Basin

Granary
Square
steps

Regent's
Canal

Viewpoint

Viewing
platform

King's
Cross
Theatre

Piccadilly line

YORK WAY

TIBER GARDENS

TIBER GARDENS

YORK WAY

Camley
Street
Natural
Park

GOODS

WAY

CAMDEN

PANCRAS
SQUARE

CRINAN STREET

N

PANCRAS

KING'S BOULEVARD

WHARFDALE ROAD

0   50 m

COACH
ROAD

GRANGER
& CO

KING'S
CROSS

RAILWAY STREET

ALBION
YARD

BALFE STREET

YORK WAY

ROAD

ALBION YARD

CALEDONIA
STREET

DRINK
SHOP
DO

TO
THE GILBERT
SCOTT &
BRITISH
LIBRARY SHOP
(SEE MAP
LEFT)

BAR
PEPITO

CALEDONIAN ROAD

ST PANCRAS
INTERNATIONAL
CONCOURSE

PANCRAS

Great
Northern
Hotel

KING'S CROSS
ST PANCRAS

Regent
Quarter

PENTONVILLE RD

ST PANCRAS
INTERNATIONAL

ROAD

SIR JOHN
BETJEMAN
STATUE

Northern line

Victoria line

EUSTON ROAD

MIDLAND RD

THE
MEETING
PLACE

GRAY'S INN
ROAD

1. BRITISH LIBRARY SHOP

96 Euston Road, NW1 2DB
020 7412 7332, shop.bl.uk
Mon, Wed–Fri 9.30am–6pm,
Tues 9.30am–8pm, Sat
9.30am–5pm, Sun 11am–5pm

The shop attached to the British Library is a treasure trove of books and gifts for the curious and literary-minded. Choose from *Alice in Wonderland* teacups and saucers or quill cufflinks, chic re-editions of classics like Jane Austen's *Persuasion* or the British Library's own mystery crime series (like the 1930s *Murder Undergound* or one of Alfred Hitchcock's favourites, *Number Seventeen*). There are also London-distilled gin, pots of gold ink (inspired by the Magna Carta, stored at the library), or reproductions of maps with such delights as a 16th century insight into celestial hemispheres or a medieval plan of the city of Jerusalem. Every purchase supports the British Library and the conservation of its archive of over 150 million items (the largest collection in the world), including manuscripts, maps and music.

2. DRINK SHOP DO

9 Caledonian Road, N1 9DX
020 7278 4335,
drinkshopdo.com
Mon–Thurs 10.30am–12am,
Fri–Sat 10.30am–2am,
Sun 10.30am–8pm

Drink Shop Do really should also have FUN, in big capital letters, incorporated into its name. The shop is an inspired idea of two best friends Kristie Bishop and Coralie Sleap, where craft workshops collide with cuppas, cakes and cocktails. Learn to embroider, macramé or screen-print while sipping a rose and lychee martini, or go along on a Friday or Saturday night for an old skool mosh up on the dance floor. Open all day (the cafe serves tea, coffee, simple toasted sandwiches, soups and homemade cake on weekdays, basic brunch and afternoon tea at weekends), part of the novelty is that everything you see is up for sale – there's plenty of jewellery, home accessories and decorative wrapping tapes and paper, all by independent designers.

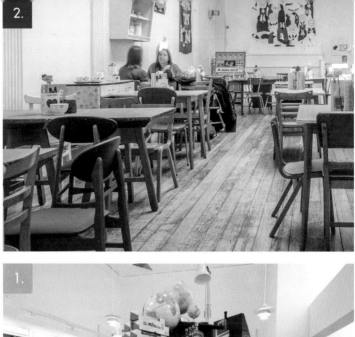

3.

GRAIN STORE

Granary Square, King's Cross,
1–3 Stable Street, N1C 4AB
020 7324 4466, grainstore.com
Mon–Wed 10am–11.30pm,
Thurs–Fri 10am–12am, Sat
10am–12am, Sun 10am–3pm

Michelin-starred chef Bruno
Loubet brings a down-
to-earth yet innovative
approach to dishes where
the vegetables, not the meat
or fish, are the star attraction.
Grain Store was one of the
first restaurants to become
part of the regenerated King's
Cross; its rustic-meets-
industrial space, designed
by Russell Sage, blurring
the lines between kitchen
and dining room. With
one eye on sustainability
and seasonality, and the
other on the memory of
vegetables from his Bordeaux
childhood, Bruno plays with
fermented, sprouting, pickled
and smoked ingredients.
Buttermilk pot-roasted
cauliflower with preserved
plum, light smoked potato
mousseline with lovage oil,
and farro wheat 'risotto' are
just some of the dishes. Go
for the veg-inspired cocktails
too – celeriac bellini, carrot
gimlet or paprika-soaked
white wine.

4.

GRANGER & CO

Unit 1 Stanley Building,
7 Pancras Square, N1C 4AG
020 3058 2567,
grangerandco.com
Mon–Sat 7am–11pm,
Sun 8am–10.30pm

Famed Aussie chef Bill
Granger brings Sydney
sunshine to the menus at his
group of London Granger &
Co restaurants. My favourite
is this one, with its Brutalist
concrete and terrazzo tile feel,
saturated with natural light
from ceiling-high windows
stretching the length of the
restaurant. Emphasis is on
light, tasty and satisfying
ingredients and flavours, with
a few of his star signature
dishes, like corn fritters and
ricotta pancakes, alongside
global-food inspired fare
like sticky chilli pork belly,
nigella-seeded tempura
courgette (zucchini) slices or
yellow fish curry. Their take
on the classic Aperol spritz
is a must (sometimes laced
with grapefruit, elderflower or
passionfruit) but be warned,
it's hard to stop at one, maybe
not such a good idea to have
more than two though.

3.

4.

4.

4.

3.

4.

5.

DISHOOM

5 Stable Street, N1C 4AB
020 7420 9321, dishoom.com
Mon–Wed 8am–11pm, Thurs–Fri
8am–12am, Sat 9am–12am,
Sun 9am–11pm

You don't often have a fresh-baked bacon naan for breakfast, but at award-winning Dishoom this is exactly the thing to order – extra delicious thanks to renowned Marylebone butcher The Ginger Pig's moreish salty and sweet dry-cured streaky rashers – enjoyed along with a pungent, chocolatey Monsooned Malabar coffee or spicy House chai. Here, in this converted three-storey Victorian railway transit shed, the mood is sultry, romantic 1920s' old Bombay; the name derived from the 'dishoom dishoom' sound effect of classic fight scene blows in a Bollywood musical. With a bowl of 'Far Far' (a colourful salty, lemony crispy snack), try a Viceroy's Old Fashioned (aged bourbon muddled with a bay leaf reduction and green tea), before tantalising the tastebuds with family-recipe chicken tikka, 24-hour cooked black lentil daal and chicken cranberry 'Britannia' biryani.

THE GILBERT SCOTT

St Pancras Renaissance Hotel,
Euston Road, NW1 2AR
020 7278 3888,
thegilbertscott.co.uk
Bar: Mon–Fri 11am–late, Sat–
Sun 10am–late; restaurant:
Mon–Fri 12–3pm & 5.30–11pm,
Sat 12–11pm, Sun 12–9pm

Heading to Paris via the Eurostar is always more exciting with a quick pit stop at glamorous Gilbert Scott before boarding. Up the sweeping front steps from Euston Road into the entrance of the captivating Gothic red-bricked St Pancras Hotel (designed by George Gilbert Scott, the leading architect of his day), top British chef Marcus Wareing oversees the brasserie-style restaurant's menu of rich traditional English fare, such as ribs of beef, saddleback pork chops and rabbit pie. There's a thrill to sliding into one of the leather banquettes in the romantically lit and deep red bar, with a glass of West Sussex Nyetimber sparkling rosé and a little plate of crispy cod cheeks. It's a great place for weekend brunch too, try the Dorset crab 'Benedict' or the smokey haddock omelette Arnold Bennett.

St Pancras International is a wonder of Victorian engineering and Gothic architecture; the poet Sir John Betjeman helped save it from demolition in the 1960s and there's a statue of him, created by Martin Jennings, on the upper concourse. Nearby, admire the 9-metre tall bronze sculpture *The Meeting Place* (known as 'The Lovers') by artist Paul Day, and the station's iconic large clock handmade by watchmakers Dent. **King's Cross Station** has a magical lattice-worked vaulted ceiling in the western concourse; and the **Great Northern** and **St Pancras Renaissance** hotels have been restored to their lavish former glories.

Literary and history buffs must visit the **British Library** (96 Euston Road, NW1 2DB, bl.uk) – book ahead for access to one of its 11 reading rooms with subjects from archaeology to zoology alongside a fantastic sound archive (they even have Beatles' manuscripts) and Leonardo da Vinci's notebooks.

The **House of Illustration** (2 Granary Square, King's Cross, N1C 4BH, houseofillustration.org.uk), founded by Sir Quentin Blake (most famous for his collaboration with Roald Dahl), is a neat, sweet little museum dedicated to illustration (from advertising and animation to fashion design and children's books). It hosts exhibitions and talks, and has a charming shop.

At the **Camley Street Natural Park** (12 Camley Street, N1C 4PW, kingscross.co.uk), take time out to enjoy a wetland, woodland and meadow refuge for urban birds, butterflies and bats.

KING'S CROSS LOCAL RECOMMENDS

The King's Cross branch is the third London outpost for Aussie restaurateur **Bill Granger**'s Granger & Co.

Kings Place
(90 York Way): Sit with a coffee or drink as you watch life go by on the Great Western Union Canal towpath, before attending a music recital, author talk or comedy night at this world-class arts venue.

The Lexington (96–98 Pentonville
Road): A fab spot for a craft beer and juicy burger before a gig upstairs in the intimate performance space which hosts rising talent and warm-up sessions for bigger acts.

St Pancras International
Concourse: Pop in for a great mix of British fashion (Joules, LK Bennett and Thomas Pink), gifts (Hamley's, Oliver Bonas and Apsinal of London) and fresh food (Sourced Market, M&S).

Bar Pepito (3 Varnishers Yard): I love
a glass of fine La Bota Fino sherry with some acorn-fed Andalusian Ibérico ham and Cádiz goat's cheese with moscatel grapes.

Camden Passage (Camden
Passage, Angel, Islington): Here I love to satisfy my weakness for vintage bread-boards and antique silver serving spoons and contemporary ceramics in the little shops lining these historic passages.

Barry's (163 Euston Road): When I'm
in need of a quick body burn, I book in for an intense workout at Barry's.

CLERKENWELL

Clerkenwell was once a strange no-man's-land, the conduit between the Bloomsbury borders of the West End and the grittiness of Old Street to the east. Now it has flourished as a design destination for big and small furniture brands, with the annual design show Clerkenwell London each May, and a hub for emerging craftspeople. It's also a great place to eat, drink and shop.

Whether it's the popular pedestrianised hub of **Exmouth Market** (*see* page 092), seeking out vintage homewares on Clerkenwell Road or sharing a great meal with friends along St John Street, this precinct is a hipster haven.

TO
MAP RIGHT
(VIA OLD STREET
& CLERKENWELL
ROAD)

24   JUN 8016

SHOP
1 MARBY & ELM
2 SCP
3 IN WITH THE OLD
SHOP AND EAT
4 CLERKENWELL LONDON
5 THE QUALITY CHOP HOUSE

17

EAT
THE MODERN PANTRY
EAT AND DRINK
JERUSALEM TAVERN
BOURNE & HOLLINGSWORTH
BUILDINGS

MERLIN STREET
AMWELL STREET
AVENUE
MYDDLETON STREET
GLOUCESTER WAY
WHISKIN STREET
ST JOHN STREET
WYCLIE STREET

Northampton Square

Wilmington Square

TYSOE STREET

FINSBURY

MEREDITH STREET

Islington Museum

ROSEBERY
FAMILY TREE
EXMOUTH MARKET

PERCIVAL ST

BOURNE & HOLLINGSWORTH BUILDINGS

SKINNER STREET

ST JOHN STREET

AGDON STREET

EC ONE

IN WITH THE OLD
MORO
MORITO
CONTENT & CO

Spa Fields Park

WOODBRIDGE STREET

CORPORATION ROW

CARAVAN
PINE STREET

NORTHAMPTON

ROAD

ISLINGTON

ST JOHN STREET

PAESAN

THE QUALITY CHOP HOUSE

GREEN LANE

CLERKENWELL CLOSE

SANS

ST JAMES'S WALK

SEKFORDE STREET

HAYWARD'S PLACE

STREET

GAZZANO'S

CLERKENWELL LONDON

THE EAGLE
Eagle Gallery

BOWLING

PEARTREE COURT

CLERKENWELL

CLERKENWELL

St James Church
The Crypt Theatre

AYLESBURY STREET

CRAWFORD PASSAGE

FARRINGDON

FARRINGDON

CLERKENWELL LANE

CLOSE
Marx Memorial Library

THE ZETTER TOWNHOUSE

TO SCP (SEE MAP LEFT)

BAKERS ROW

WARNER STREET

RAY STREET

ROAD

CLERKENWELL GREEN

THE MODERN PANTRY

SUMMERS STREET

HERBAL HILL

BACK HILL

Thameslink

CRAFT CENTRAL

ROAD

MARBY & ELM

CLERKENWELL ROAD

0   50 m

CLERKENWELL

ROAD

CLERKENWELL

BRITTON STREET

ONSLOW STREET

SAFFRON HILL

Hammersmith & City line

ST JOHN'S PATH

JERUSALEM TAVERN

BRISET STREET

LEATHER

WALL

HATTON

SAFFRON STREET

SAFFRON HILL

HATTON PLACE

ST CROSS STREET

Metropolitan line

TURNMILL STREET

BENJAMIN STREET

ALBION PLACE

PORTPOOL LANE

N

HATTON

ST CROSS STREET

STREET

FARRINGDON

SAFFRON

FARRINGDON RD

FARRINGDON

COWCROSS STREET

BALDWINS GARDENS

LANE

WW Contemporary Art Gallery

GARDEN

KIRBY STREET

HILL

Circle line

COWCROSS STREET

1.

MARBY & ELM

33 Clerkenwell Road,
EC1M 5RN
020 3609 9972,
marbyandelm.com
Mon–Fri 10am–6pm, Sat by
appointment

Who can resist the beauty
of a hand-pressed birthday
card or notepad? I know I
can't. Eleanor Tattersfield
has poured her love for the
art of lettering (her dad, an
acclaimed lettering artist,
was responsible for hand
painting the Cadbury's logo)
into letterpress printing with
the help of a vintage hand-
fed press. Much of what's on
sale – greeting cards, notelets
and notebooks, printed
packing tape, coasters and
stickers – are designed,
printed and packed on
site. There are also rubber
stamps that say Too Good
or Thank You, writing sets
and paperweights.

2.

SCP

135–139 Curtain Road,
EC2A 3BX
020 7739 1869, scp.co.uk
Mon–Sat 9.30am–6pm,
Sun 11am–5pm

For the past 30 years, SCP's
Sheridan Coakley has been
combining the search for
classic and rare modernist
pieces with fostering British
talent, young and old (such
as furniture designers
Matthew Hilton and Russell
Pinch, textile designers
Donna Wilson and Timorous
Beasties, and ceramicists
like Reiko Kaneko). Each
collaboration produces
pieces unique to SCP, always
with an emphasis on British-
based craftsmanship and
enduring quality. In both
this store, and its store
in Notting Hill, there's so
much to discover: chopping
boards, jugs, cushions, bottle
openers, bean bags, mobiles,
storage boxes and carved
wooden birds.

3.

IN WITH THE OLD

31 Exmouth Market, EC1R 4QL
07919 021400,
inwiththeoldshop.com
Mon 10am–7pm, Tues–Sat
10am–7.30pm, Sun
11.30am–6pm

At In With The Old, where
you're met at the door by
shop dog Goose, owner
Alice Howard is passionate
about the actual business
of making things, drawing
together work by local artists
and artisans using traditional
techniques for homewares
and accessories. There are
hand-screen printed tote bags,
laser-cut birchwood necklaces,
gift cards by Hackney printer
Bow & Arrow, vintage finds
such as stoneware pots,
own-designed collections
such as handmade jewellery
in copper and brass, Liberty
print baby shoes and
lavender heat bags, all made
on site in the downstairs
studio workshop.

CLERKENWELL LONDON

155 Farringdon Road,
EC1R 3AD
020 3826 1142,
clerkenwell-london.com
Mon–Wed 10am–6pm, Thurs–
Fri 10am–7pm, Sat 10am–5pm

This three-storey emporium
oozes good taste, with
masculine industrial lighting,
gold parquet flooring,
streamlined consoles, printed
silk cushions, credenzas
made from ethically sourced
American walnut, ceramic
and spun copper pots, even
shiny silver satchel bags,
all for sale. Try on pieces
by Zo Jordan or share a
glass of wine in the **Vinyl
Lounge** (decked out in
vintage collectables and a
custom DJ booth). Grab a
quick bite from the **155 Bar
& Kitchen**, overseen by
former Jamie Oliver Fifteen
alumnus Gavin Gordon, with
tasty dishes for breakfast,
such as house-made waffles,
bacon, scrambled egg and
shaved truffle, or for lunch, a
contemporary take on steak-
frites (Lake District Farmers'
rib eye, beef dripping chips
and fried duck egg) followed
by Williams pear trifle.

THE QUALITY CHOP HOUSE

88–94 Farringdon Road,
EC1R 3EA
020 7278 1452,
thequalitychophouse.com
Mon–Sat 12–11pm, Sun 12–4pm

The Grade II listed building
in which this restaurant,
wine bar, butchers and deli
is located dates back to 1869
(its dining room still bears the
original booth configuration),
but since re-opening in late
2012, its heart lies squarely
in a 21st century passion
for quality British produce
and a satisfying daily 'nose
to tail' menu. There are
unusual cuts like beef brisket,
Yorkshire hare or fresh-caught
Cornish cod with monk's
beard, alongside generous
chops like schnitzeled pork
or anchovy-crumbed Black
Face lamb. Carrots might
come pine-smoked, potatoes
are confited then fried, even
the butter is homemade.
They hold butchery courses
(includes three course
lunch, book ahead) or grab a
take-away treat like a fresh-
made sausage roll, sold by
the inch.

6.

THE MODERN PANTRY

47–48 St John's Square,
EC1V 4JJ
020 7553 9210,
themodernpantry.co.uk
Mon 8am–10pm, Tues–Fri 8am–
10.30pm, Sat 9am–10.30pm,
Sun 10am–10pm

Kiwi–Danish chef Anna
Hansen made her name at
Marylebone's The Providores
before setting out on her
own with The Modern Pantry
in 2008 (there's a second
restaurant in Finsbury
Square). Overlooking the
quaint cobbled St John's
Square, it's a good-value
spot any time of the day,
whether for breakfast or a
weekend brunch, or lunch
and dinner every day. Dishes
exude adventurous flavour
combinations such as
salmon sashimi teamed with
truffled mustard seed and
soy dressing, fennel flowers
and *yuzu tobiko*, smoked
burrata with muscat grapes,
or pomegranate roasted red
onions dressed with sherry
vinegar and Argan oil. Expect
unusual ingredients too,
like cassava (yucca) chips,
crunchy toasted buckwheat
and even savoury hints
of licorice.

7.

JERUSALEM TAVERN

55 Britton Street, EC1M 5UQ
020 7490 4281,
stpetersbrewery.co.uk
Mon–Fri 11am–11pm,
Sun 12–6pm

Come to the Jerusalem
Tavern, run by Suffolk
brewery St Peter's, for its
atmosphere, authenticity and
of course, the beer. With its
bare boards and cosy fire,
it's not fancy – set in a 1720
merchant's house (with a
clock workshop shopfront
added around 1810). Its
name is said to derive from
the Priory of St John of
Jerusalem, founded in 1140,
whose only surviving relic
is the nearby St John's Gate
around the corner. Samuel
Johnson, William Hogarth
and Handel are all rumoured
to have drunk here. Try a
simple but hearty sandwich,
like roast pork loin with apple
sauce on sourdough to help
keep you downing those
Ruby red ales by moody
candlelight all night.

BOURNE & HOLLINGSWORTH BUILDINGS

42 Northampton Road,
EC1R 0HU
020 3174 1156,
bandhbuildings.com
Mon–Thurs 11am–12am, Fri
11am–1am, Sat 10am–1am,
Sun 10am–6pm

The fickle fashionista in me couldn't care less if the food and drink were no good here (although thankfully they are) – it's just so darn pretty, and a great place to be the minute you step over the threshold. With its mix of cane furniture and antique garden chairs, hanging baskets and giant ferns, and vintage armchairs upholstered in tropical flora and foliage, it's the place to come for a weekend brunch of *Huevos Benedictos* – chorizo, avocado, béarnaise sauce and *pico de gallo* (salsa). Or come for cocktail hour and try a Quincey Collins – gin shaken with quince liqueur, fresh lemon juice and a touch of sugar served long with soda – and a side of battered parsnip chips with honey rosemary dip.

Exmouth Market has top Italian home cooking at **Paesan** and global fare at **Caravan**. Find handcrafted accessories at **Family Tree**, the hottest jewellery designers at **EC One** and hipster fashion at **Content & Co**.

Around the corner, for inspiring contemporary ballet (featuring world-leading visiting dance companies with tickets at affordable prices), don't miss **Sadlers Wells** (Rosebery Avenue, EC1R 4TN, sadlerswells.com).

On Clerkenwell Road, discover vintage homewares at **Forest London** and emerging makers at **Craft Central**. Enjoy fried chilli corn and a Peach Leaf Fizz in the bar at **The Zetter Townhouse** or catch a gig over spicy voodoo chicken wings and bottles of ale at **The Slaughtered Lamb** (34–35 Great Sutton Street). For foodies, the 'nose to tail' cooking at **St John** (26 St John Street) is a must. At the end of the street, historic **Smithfield Markets** still bustles as a wholesale meat market.

The Brutalist-designed **Barbican Centre** (Silk Street, EC2Y 8DS, barbican.org.uk), built in the 1980s with its urban mix of residential, commercial and cultural living, is one of my favourite spots in London. It's a fantastic venue for music gigs (and home to the London Symphony Orchestra), plays, exhibitions and indie films; its food-hall-style cafe serves delicious food and the indoor tropical garden, complete with exotic fish, is one of the city's best hidden treasures (open Sundays only).

Chef **Anna Hansen** opened The Modern Pantry in 2008.

The Quality Chop House Shop (*see* page 086): I'm always looking out for really interesting ingredients from around the world, and here I pick up a block of Shaun Searley's super short suet and butter crust pastry (look in the freezer), perfect for anything savoury such as sausage rolls.

Gazzano's (167–169 Farringdon Road): Here I buy the Tuscan fennel seed sausages and lardo, which I slice thinly and serve on warm bruschetta.

Caravan (11–13 Exmouth Market): No one does better coffee in London than Caravan – so much so, we actually serve their coffee at The Modern Pantry!

Moro (34–36 Exmouth Market): I like the abundance of Middle Eastern and Mediterranean ingredients that Moro puts together, like the wood-roasted skate with spiced cauliflower, roasted chickpeas and tahini sauce. Morito, their restaurant next door, is a fun place to grab a sherry and share a few tapas plates.

The Eagle (159 Farringdon Road): London's original gastro pub, serving hearty British food that's not fussy but great quality, and consistently good service. I particularly like the free range pork belly with borlotti beans and salsa verde.

The East End's innovative young chefs, designers and craftspeople have transformed this precinct into one of London's most exciting food and design destinations, oozing with an experimental and edgy vibe that's also upbeat and welcoming.

Wander around **Spitalfields markets** (dating back to 1666), and explore the rising talent and innovative craftsmanship in boutiques and cafes on Redchurch, Rivington, Curtain and Shoreditch High streets. There's an emphasis on great British design along **Calvert Avenue**, and 'Curry Mile' **Brick Lane** hosts vintage, artisan, designer and food markets on weekends at the **Old Truman Brewery**.

HACKNEY
ROAD
ALLGOOD STREET
HORATIO
THE MARKSMAN
BATH
GROVE
CADELL
CLOSE
STREET
STREET
SHIPTON
RAVENSCROFT
JONES DAIRY
NELLY DUFF
EZRA STREET
ROAD
BOB & BLOSSOM
Ravenscroft Park
SUCK & CHEW
STREET
FLOWER MARKET
COLUMBIA
Jesus Green
REBECCA LOUISE LAW
ELWIN
NÔM
TO MAP RIGHT
QUILTER STREET
STREET
ANGELA FLANDERS
THE BIRDCAGE
WELLINGTON
ROW
GOSSET
STREET

SHOP
1 CHARLENE MULLEN
2 HOUSE OF HACKNEY
3 LABOUR AND WAIT
4 MAST BROS
5 AIDA

24   JUN 8OT6

SPITALFIELDS AND SHOREDITCH

SHOP, EAT AND DRINK
BARBER & PARLOUR
COLUMBIA ROAD
EAT
ROCHELLE CANTEEN
EAT AND DRINK
HACKNEY AND DALSTON

17

TO
HACKNEY AND
DALSTON
(NOT SHOWN
ON MAP)

KINGSLAND ROAD

COLUMBIA ROAD

BAKERS RENTS

HACKNEY ROAD

GASCOIGNE PLACE

TO
COLUMBIA
ROAD
(SEE MAP
LEFT)

SHOREDITCH

AUSTIN STREET

VIRGINIA ROAD

SWANFIELD STREET

HOUSE OF
HACKNEY

St Leonards
Church

BOUNDARY STREET

VIRGINIA ROAD

HOCKER STREET

TOWER
HAMLETS

8
AIDA

CHARLENE
MULLEN

CALVERT

AVENUE

O'DELL'S

Boundary
Gardens
ARNOLD
CIRCUS

PALISSY STREET

ROCHELLE STREET

STREET

SHOREDITCH

BOUNDARY STREET

Ace Hotel
London
Shoreditch

NAVARRE STREET

STREET

CLUB ROW

ROCHELLE
CANTEEN

MONTCLARE STREET

FRENCH PLACE

LIGONIER STREET

CAMLET STREET

STREET

ANNING STREET

HIGH

STREET

OLD

NICHOL

LABOUR
AND WAIT

NEW INN YARD

MAST
BROTHERS

LE LABO

STREET

BURRO E
SALVIA

CHANCE STREET

WHITBY STREET

BARBER &
PARLOUR

REDCHURCH

EBOR STREET

STREET

ROAD

London Overground

HOLYWELL
LANE

BETHNAL GREEN

SCLATER STREET

STREET

BOXPARK
Shoreditch

FAIRCHILD
STREET

GREAT EASTERN STREET

0   50 m

Central line

SHOREDITCH
HIGH STREET

N

PLOUGH YARD

West Anglia main line

Great Eastern Railway

1.
CHARLENE MULLEN
7 Calvert Avenue, E2 7JP
020 7739 6987,
charlenemullen.com
Tues–Sat 11am–6pm,
Sun 11am–5pm

Inside sought-after textile designer Charlene Mullen's smartly painted Victorian double-fronted store on the plane-tree lined Calvert Avenue, the space that is both shop and studio resonates with her signature palette of black, white and red (even down to the floor tiles, made in Morocco to Charlene's specific design). On show are prints, cushions, Dualit toasters and lampshades either hand-embroidered or printed with Charlene's illustrations – folk art daisies, sunbursts, sequin owls sitting in family trees, London, Paris and New York city scenes – alongside her tableware for Royal Doulton (illustrated with London landmarks, from red buses to the Gherkin) and amusing cat-shaped doorstops. Blankets by Eleanor Pritchard, pewter by Miranda Watkins and ceramics by Owen Wall and Daniel Reynolds complete the scene.

2.
HOUSE OF HACKNEY
131 Shoreditch High Street,
E1 6JE
020 7739 3901,
houseofhackney.com
Mon–Sat 10am–7pm,
Sun 11am–5pm

House of Hackney is an immersive bombardment of the senses as you step over the threshold and soak up the mood of slightly hedonistic, bygone grandeur with husband-and-wife team Javvy M Royle and Frieda Gormley's richly coloured, flamboyant prints which most certainly echo odes of inspiration to legendary 19th century British artist William Morris – they recently designed a fashion and homewares collection featuring a re-sized, re-coloured, re-imagined interpretation of his signature prints. Wild, over-abundant motifs such as palm fronds, tea roses and flamingoes to acanthus leaves, passion flowers, leopard stripes and panther spots bring everything from dresses and lampshades, dinner plates and deck chairs, even Puma trainers, to vivid life. Great gifts to take home include wash bags and scarves, notebooks and pencil cases.

3.

LABOUR AND WAIT

85 Redchurch Street, E2 7DJ
020 7729 6253,
labourandwait.co.uk
Tues–Sun 11am–6pm

Labour and Wait's utilitarian chic ethos is right at home in hipster, design-conscious Shoreditch. Located in what was a former pub, still pleasingly clad in its lovely original green tiles, founding duo Rachel Wythe-Moran and Simon Watkins firmly believe the things we buy and use should get better with age. Here, form and function have come together to create the best tools for making life not only easier but more joyful. On the surface, these are just ordinary things – brooms, dustpans, pegs, brushes, enamel pans, brown betty teapots, preserving jars, can openers, trowels and bird whistles – but each has been elevated, through thoughtful, pared back design, to become an enduring classic in its own right.

4.

MAST BROTHERS

19–29 Redchurch Street, E2 7DJ
020 7739 1236,
mastbrothers.com
Mon–Fri 11am–7pm, Sat–Sun 10am–7pm

The tall and long red-bearded Brooklyn brothers Rick and Michael Mast brought their pursuit for chocolate-making perfection to this gallery-style 'factory' in 2015, designed with floor-to-ceiling glass panes so customers can see the mastery at play. Beans sourced directly from small producers are roasted, tempered and set into bars on site, elevating our universal addiction for the sweet stuff to a whole new level of sensory overload. There are bars infused with sea salt or smoke, olive oil or maple; there's chocolate made with Italian sheep's milk or Dutch goat's milk; and they've even worked out a way to brew a pint of (non-alcoholic) chocolate beer which you can enjoy instore whilst trying to make the painful decision of which beautifully-decorated bars to take home with you.

5.

AIDA

133 Shoreditch High Street,
E1 6JE
020 7739 2811,
aidashoreditch.co.uk
Mon–Sat 10am–7pm,
Sun 12–6pm

Run by four sisters, the store affectionately named after their Nan, Aida is a new breed of independent stores, bringing fashion, lifestyle, food and music together under one roof. It has a warehouse feel of exposed brick walls and painted floors, and independent European and local labels. There are handcrafted canvas and leather satchels, striped cotton tees, checked shirts and suave Derby lace-ups for boys; great rain macs and printed trousers, metallic loafers and vintage-inspired watches for girls. For the home, there are hammam cotton throws and hand-thrown bowls. Stop at the cafe for treats and a coffee, or book for a vintage make-up makeover in Aida's Parlour. In the evenings, Aida live sessions give rising young musicians an arena to play their music.

6.

BARBER & PARLOUR

64–66 Redchurch Street,
E2 7DP
020 3376 1777,
barberandparlour.com
Mon–Sat 9am–11pm,
Sun 10am–11pm

You can live out an entire day at Barber & Parlour – stretching across a whole block of hipper than hip Shoreditch. There's a relaxed cafe on the ground floor – grab a BBQ pulled pork bun with apple, fennel and celeriac slaw and pickles on the side, with a fresh pressed House juice – and then prepare to be pampered. If your 'tache is in need of a trim or you fancy a grade one buzz cut all over, head to **Neville Barber**, (they do a traditional wet shave too); for a glossy cut, colour or blow-dry, head upstairs to **Cheeky Hair By Josh Wood**; and for pretty pinkies, the **Cheeky Parlour** will do the trick. A lime and ginger infused vodka Soho Mule will get you in the mood before heading to the in-house **Electric Cinema**, complete with deep leather armchairs, table lamps and blankets, for the latest movie blockbuster.

5.

5.

6.

5.

5.

6.

7.

COLUMBIA ROAD

On Sundays, head out early to make the most of the colours, smells and atmosphere of Columbia Road's noisy, happy, heart-lifting **flower market** and grab a delicious coffee and breakfast bap from **Jones Dairy**. Even if you can't take home a bunch of flowers, enjoy exploring the hundreds of blooms, bulbs, shrubs and potted perennials on show. Enjoy the lively banter as stallholders, some in weekly residence for more than 40 years, shout out daily specials. There are interesting independent shops too (most open daily) – a favourite is finding limited edition works by new artists at **Nelly Duff**. There's perfume by **Angela Flanders**, floral installations and prints by **Rebecca Louise Law**, old-fashioned sweeties at **Suck & Chew**, Vietnamese and Cambodian homewares at **Nôm**, and groovy kidswear and toys at **Bob & Blossom**. After all the foraging, quench your thirst with a pint at **The Birdcage** or enjoy a full-blown, delicious Sunday roast at **The Marksman**.

ROCHELLE CANTEEN

Rochelle School, Arnold Circus,
E2 7ES
020 7729 5677,
arnoldandhenderson.com
Mon–Fri 9am–4.30pm

New Zealand–born Margot Henderson oversees the seasonal menu at Rochelle Canteen, located in the converted bike shed of an old Victorian school, secluded from the Shoreditch streets by a pretty walled garden. The garden is a particularly glorious spot to sit when the sun is shining and the birds are singing. Food is hearty and plentiful and changes for mood and season – slow-roasted joints with fresh bitter leaf salads, rillettes with pickled fruits, hearty classics like coq au vin or lemon sole with capers, parsley and brown butter. Follow with baked cheese and salad for two, crumbles with jersey cream or blood orange and almond cake. Wine is BYO.

9

HACKNEY AND DALSTON

Beyond Shoreditch, areas like Hackney and Dalston have blossomed. On weekends, head to **Broadway Market** for delicious treats including **Knead**'s flavoured crumpets and Claire Ptak's **Violet Bakery** (photos this page top, 9D and F) sweet treats (she also has a cafe in Hackney Downs). Great pubs include **The Cat & Mutton** and the Arts and Crafts style **The Dove**. Around Bethnal Green, there are cutting-edge dishes and unusual wines at **Sager + Wilde** (193 Hackney Road, photos this page bottom, 9B and C) and its sister venue **Paradise Row** (Arch 250 Paradise Row, photo 9A), **Typing Room** and **Corner Room** restaurants at the Town Hall Hotel, and **Bistrotheque** (23–27 Wadeson Street, photo 9E). Savour an on-site brew at London Fields Brewery's **Taproom** (365–366 Warburton Street). For an evolutionary history of British interiors, visit the **Geffrey Museum** (136 Kingsland Road); stop by **Whitechapel Gallery** (77–82 Whitechapel High Street) for contemporary art, photography and multimedia installations.

9A.

9B.

9C.

9D.

9E.

9F.

Spitalfields markets and its surrounding squares include highlights such as Brit chocolatier **Montezuma's**, jeweller **Dower & Hall** and fashion at **McQ by Alexander McQueen**. Brasseries such as **Galvin HOP** and **Blixen** bustle all day long, and there's Nuno Mendes's Portuguese flavours at **Taberna Do Mercado**. You can easily while away the hours scouring the ever-evolving daily stalls of fashion, art, antiques and vinyl records. At weekends, the vintage stalls along **Brick Lane** are the place to be.

Dennis Severs House
(18 Folgate Street, E1 6BX, dennissevershouse.co.uk) is an unusual adventure through ten candlelit rooms, depicting the lives of an 18th century family of Huguenot silk-weavers who originally lived in the house. As you wander through the rooms, a series of sounds, textures and smells encourage you to become part of the narrative. It's an immersive experience, an opportunity to become lost in another time.

Kids big and small will love the 400-year-old collection of childhood toys, games, clothing and paraphernalia like school work and reports at the V&A's offshoot **Museum of Childhood** (Cambridge Heath Road, E2 9PA, vam.ac.uk), which gives an intriguing insight into the way different children have lived since the 1600s.

Charlene Mullen opened her store in 2013.

Hoxton Street Monster Supplies (159 Hoxton Street): I love the great branding of sweets sold here – Cubed Earwax (toffees), Tinned Fear (boiled sweets) – which come with specially commissioned stories aimed at encouraging young people to read and write fiction. All profits go to supporting leading author Nick Hornby's Ministry of Stories children's creative writing charity.

Fabrique (Arch 385, Geffrye Street): A Swedish bakery making fantastic bread and cinnamon buns to die for just by Hoxton Market.

O'Dell's (24 Calvert Avenue): Owner Tom O'Dell has great style, selling a great mix of gifts, candles, menswear, planters, and chopping boards.

Le Labo (61 Redchurch Street): This is a beautiful store with the best orange scent, Fleur D'Oranger 27, ever.

Burro e Salvia (52 Redchurch Street): They make wonderful fresh pasta, hold pasta courses and you can eat there too – it's all delicious and it looks beautiful.

Beigel Bake (159 Brick Lane): Open 24 hours, this bagel bakery makes bagels in the traditional Jewish way with fillings like hot salt beef, smoked salmon and cream cheese. It's been there forever and they still make the best bagels at the best price. Great for when I'm in a rush.

London Bridge is where historical 13th century landmarks like **Southwark Cathedral** and Borough Market (*see* page 110) mix with strikingly contemporary architecture including Norman Foster's **City Hall** (home to the Mayor of London) and the gleaming 95-storey glass facade of **The Shard** (*see* page 114).

Visit **HMS** *Belfast*, now a naval museum, moored on the Thames, or adventure across **Tower Bridge**, still a functioning 'bascule' (drawbridge), via its 42-metre-high glass walkways to reach the **Tower of London** (home to the Crown jewels) on the other side. **Potter's Field Park** makes a great spot to sit with a take-away sandwich and coffee from the many foodie providores nearby.

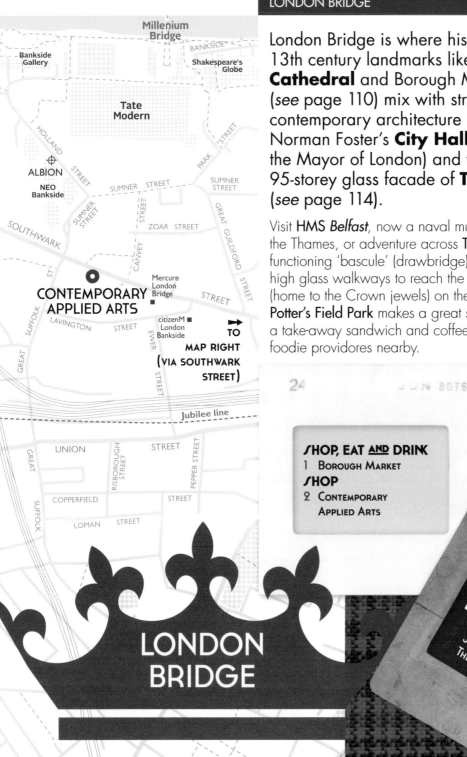

SHOP, EAT AND DRINK
1 BOROUGH MARKET
SHOP
2 CONTEMPORARY APPLIED ARTS

EAT
ELLIOT'S
EAT AND DRINK
THE SHARD
JOSÉ TAPAS BAR
THE GEORGE INN

LONDON BRIDGE

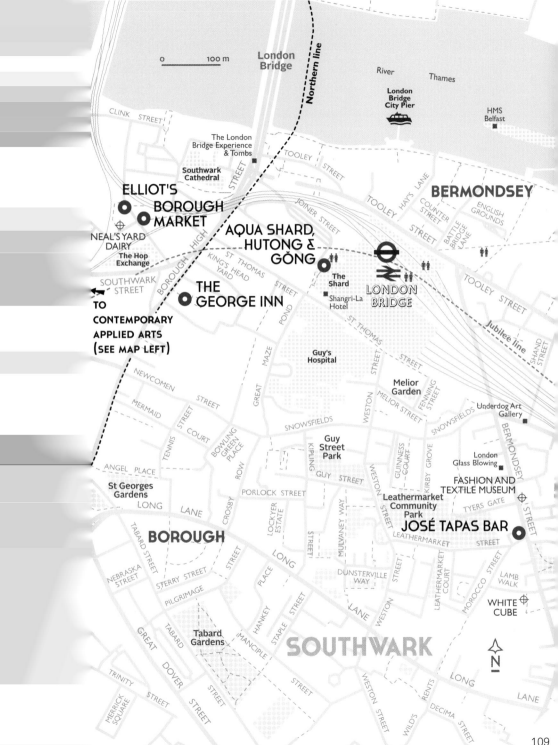

BOROUGH MARKET

8 Southwark Street, SE1 1TL
020 7407 1002,
boroughmarket.org.uk
Mon–Tues (lunch only) 10am–5pm
Full market: Wed–Thurs
10am–5pm, Fri 10am–6pm,
Sat 8am–5pm

No self-respecting foodie should miss Borough Market, London's oldest fresh food market, dating back to the 13th century. It's a mouth-watering mix of produce: fresh fruit, vegetables, meat, fish, and breads, cakes, cheese, and great coffee. There are truffle-infused oils, honeys, licorice marinades, gluten-free breads, and lunchtime baguettes bursting with roast pork, stuffing and apple sauce. Try every oyster under the sun at **Wright Brothers**, award-winning salted caramel doughnuts at **Bread Ahead** and a glass of Puglian Moscato at **Bedales**. **Rabot 1745** (flagship store for Hotel Chocolat, photos 1B and D) is a chocoholic's dream. Find regional Spanish ingredients and tapas at **Brindisa** (photos 1A and C) or Lebanese kibbeh, borekas and stuffed pides at **Arabica**. For the true gourmand, join a gastrotour with **Celia Brooks** (celiabrooks.com). Finish with a fresh-made scoop of rhubarb sorbet from **Gelateria 3Bis**.

1A.

1B.

1C.

1.

1.

1D.

2.

CONTEMPORARY APPLIED ARTS

89 Southwark Street, SE1 0HX
020 7620 0086, caa.org.uk
Mon–Sat 10am–6pm

Contemporary Applied Arts (CAA) has been championing and promoting British craft since the late 1940s – hotelier and interior designer Kit Kemp is a huge fan of commissioning designer–makers from its rollcall of members to create unique pieces for her hotels. In this light-filled space, you'll find one-off works to suit all budgets, from established names like world-renowned glass artist Peter Layton to rising-star potter Billy Lloyd. A whole spectrum of materials is at play here – from wood and metal, to upcycled paper and cloth, glass and acrylic; multimedia pieces combining anything from digital photography to fishing line wire; and hand thrown stone- and celadon-ware to paper-thin porcelain.

3.

ELLIOT'S

12 Stoney Street, Borough
Market, SE1 9AD
020 7403 7436, elliotscafe.com
Mon–Fri 12–3pm & 6–10pm,
Sat 12–4pm & 6–10pm

The day starts early for the
team at Elliot's – its highly
reputable chewy, crusty bread
is made and ingredients for
their menu are foraged from
the market's fresh food stalls.
A new season's arrival can
inspire Aussie owner and
chef Brett Redman to create
a complete menu change
twice a day (he also has a
hand in The Richmond pub
in Hackney and yakitori
restaurant Jidori in Dalston).
Food oozes a clean freshness,
from wood-fire grilled, dry-
aged T-bone steaks (to share),
fresh-caught fish, healthy
shaved salads; the house
soufflé or cheddarey puffs are
made from cheeses sourced
at the renowned **Neal's Yard
Dairy** around the corner.
The burgers are an absolute,
mouth-melting must. An
entirely biodynamic wine list,
sourced from small artisan
growers, completes the as-
nature-intended appeal.

4.

THE SHARD

The Shard, 31 St Thomas Street, SE1 9RY

Aqua: 020 3011 1256, aquashard.co.uk
Mon–Fri 7am–5pm & 6pm–1am, Sat–Sun 9am–10am & 10.30am–2am

Hutong: 020 3011 1257, hutong.co.uk
Mon–Sun 12–2.30pm & 6–10.30pm; bar Mon–Thurs 12pm–12am, Fri–Sat 12pm–2am

Gŏng: 0207 234 8208, gong-shangri-la.com
Mon–Sat 12pm–1am, Sun 12pm–12am

There are spectacular views from The Shard, London's highest skyscraper. **Aqua Shard** (Level 31, photos this page top, 4B and F) is pure James Bond glamour, with its double-height glass-and-steel interiors, a contemporary British menu and aptly named cocktails such as the Belvedere 007 Martini. At **Hutong** (Level 33, photos this page bottom, 4A, C, D and E), the mood and food are inspired by the opulent surroundings in the Pekinese imperial palaces; try the lunchtime yum cha experience, with wasabi shrimp dumpling, braised beef with ginger and chef's special pickled vegetable fried rice. Or enjoy a gin-infused Bermondsey Bubbles overlooking the infinity pool at The Shangri-La Hotel's **Gŏng** (Level 52) Champagne and cocktail bar.

4A.

4B.

4C.

4D.

4E.

4F.

JOSÉ TAPAS BAR

104 Bermondsey Street,
SE1 3UB
020 7403 4902,
josepizarro.com
Mon–Sat 12–11.15pm
(last orders), Sun 12–5.15pm
(last orders)

José Pizarro, former head chef
for Brindisa, has two thriving
joints on Bermondsey
Street – José Tapas Bar and
Pizarro. Emphasis at José is
on simple, straightforward
dishes (much like its rustic
decor) but with plenty of
fresh, punchy flavours – the
crispy then creamy croquetas
and sweet, delicate vinegar
marinated boquerones
(anchovies) are a specialty,
especially when enjoyed
with a cheeky little glass (or
two) of one of Jerez's finest
sherries. Turn up early to get
a seat, otherwise it'll just be
standing room at the bar.

THE GEORGE INN

The George Inn Yard,
75–77 Borough High Street,
SE1 1NH
020 7407 2056,
george-southwark.co.uk
Mon–Sat 11am–11pm (kitchen
closes 10pm), Sun 12–10.30pm
(kitchen closes 9pm)

London Bridge was
Shakespeare's playground
(The Globe theatre, *see*
page 118, is a short walk
away) so for fans of the Bard,
step back in time at the
17th century George Inn,
now owned by the National
Trust and the city's last
remaining coaching inn
(also mentioned in Charles
Dickens' *Little Dorrit*).
Apparently Winston Churchill
dined here, so too Princess
Margaret who caused a stir
when her Sunday lunch with
the Bishop of Southwark
continued long past closing
time. Whether seated in one
of its cosy wood-panelled
nooks or outside in the
courtyard, enjoy a pint of
Olde Trip or London Glory
along with British classics
like sausage and mash or
George beef pie.

Come to the new **Shakespeare's Globe** (21 New Globe Walk, Bankside, SE1 9DT, shakespearesglobe.com) to see how it was performed in the Bard's day (they showcase new writing too). It opened first in 1997 with an outdoor theatre (performances held April–October), and expanded in 2014 with the intimate, candlelit indoor Sam Wanamaker Playhouse (productions all year). It stands just a few hundred yards from its original site.

You can't miss the brightly coloured facade of the **Fashion and Textile Museum** (83 Bermondsey Street, SE1 3XF, ftmlondon.org), founded by fashion designer Zandra Rhodes. Intelligent, thoughtfully curated exhibitions trace the vibrancy and joy of fashion, from celebrating pattern makers Missoni and Liberty to exalted designers Thea Porter and Bill Gibb.

Jay Jopling opened his first **White Cube** gallery (144–152 Bermondsey Street, SE1 3TQ, whitecube.com) in St James's in 1993 – bringing some of the most dynamic British artists to the fore, from Tracey Emin and Antony Gormley to Lucian Freud. Here, in White Cube's latest 58,000 square foot (5,388 square metres) gallery, it's an exciting venue for experimental exhibitions, major retrospectives, education seminars, films and a bookshop.

Shad Thames (street) is a pretty spot for lunch or dinner, especially under the twinkling lights of Tower Bridge at night. Try **The Butlers Wharf Chop House** or **Blueprint Café**. For a memorable cocktail experience, try **Bermondsey Arts Club**, a former public loo turned elegant Art Deco speakeasy bar.

Chef **Brett Redman** opened his first restaurant Elliot's in 2011.

Richard Haward's Oysters (Borough Market – Stoney Street): I love these wild oysters, fished from Richard's own tidal water beds in the River Blackwater in Essex. It gives them a much richer, denser taste than farmed oysters. Grab a dozen oysters and wine to share.

Mons Cheesemongers (Borough Market – Three Crown Square): I can't resist the *Vacherin Mont D'Or* from this second-generation French cheesemaker, who ripens their cheeses in the family's cellars based in the Loire's St Haon le Chatel.

40 Maltby Street (40 Maltby Street): I try not to work Saturday night so I can come here for proper good food by chef Stephen Williams and wines grown by small producers eschewing the use of chemicals.

Menier Chocolate Factory (53 Southwark Street): If I get the chance to escape the kitchen, this is a great place for intimate, innovative theatre performances, with many of its productions so good they transfer to the West End.

Kappacasein (Borough Market – Jubilee Place): Come here for the best *raclette* (using a special cheese – developed by stall owner Bill Oglethorpe with Somerset dairy farmer Jamie Montgomery – melted on new potatoes, baby gherkins and picked onions) or toasted cheese sandwich (Montgomery cheddar, onions, leeks and garlic on Poilâne).

Exploring the South Bank is a must for culture buffs. Stroll past the **London Eye** (*see* page 130) and you'll find the **Southbank Centre** (*see* page 123) alive with galleries, auditoriums and quality chain shops, restaurants and bars. The most vibrant arts precinct in the UK, this is where annual events like Meltdown, Womad and the London Literature Festival are held.

Next door you'll find the **British Film Institute** (*see* page 130), and then the **National Theatre** (*see* page 130). Passing by **Coin Street** gardens, the **Oxo Tower** (*see* page 130) and **Sea Containers House**, head under Blackfriars Bridge to reach the **Tate Modern** (*see* page 130) for world-class artworks.

SHOP
1 SNOWDEN FLOOD
SHOP AND EAT
2 SOUTHBANK CENTRE
EAT
3 THE ANCHOR & HOPE

EAT AND DRINK
SKYGARDEN
THE FOUNDERS ARMS
WAHACA
DRINK
DANDELYAN

SOUTH BANK

Map labels:

Threadneedles Hotel
LEADENHALL STREET
CORNHILL
CITY OF LONDON
FENCHURCH ST
TO MAP RIGHT (VIA QUEEN VICTORIA & CANNON STREETS)
LIME STREET
FENCHURCH STREET
SKYGARDEN
CRUTCHED FRIARS
MARK LANE
SEETHING LANE
TOWER HILL
Circle line
District line
MONUMENT
DLR
LOWER THAMES STREET
Tower of London
London Bridge City Pier
River Thames
HMS Belfast
Tower Pier
HAY'S LANE
Hays Galleria
TOOLEY STREET
City Hall
Potters Fields Park
SHAND STREET
Jubilee line
LONDON BRIDGE
Guy's Hospital
SNOWSFIELDS
BERMONDSEY STREET
WESTON STREET
TOWER BRIDGE ROAD

TO
SKYGARDEN
(SEE MAP LEFT)

St Dunstan-in-the-West

FLEET   STREET
STRAND
FLEET STREET
ALDWYCH
CLEMENTS INN

Apex
Temple
Court
Hotel

WHITEFRIARS STREET
BOUVERIE STREET
TUDOR   STREET
CARMELITE STREET
JOHN CARPENTER STREET

QUEEN   VICTORIA   ST

Inner
Temple
Gardens

CROWN OFFICE ROW

Roman
Bath

Circle line

BLACKFRIARS

VICTORIA
EMBANKMENT   District line

TEMPLE

HQS
Wellington

HMS
President

Blackfriars
Millenium
Pier

BLACKFRIARS
BRIDGE

THE
FOUNDERS
ARMS

Thames

River

0   100 m

SNOWDEN
FLOOD

WAGUMI

DANDELYAN

Sea
Containers

BANKSIDE
GALLERY

GROUND

WATERLOO
BRIDGE

GABRIEL'S
WHARF

Bernie
Spain
Gardens

Upper

BROADWALL

STAMFORD
STREET

RENNIE STREET
HOPTON STREET
HOLLAND STREET

SOUTH
BANK

National
Theatre

GROUND

DUCHY

ALBION

THE QUEEN'S WALK

UPPER

COIN STREET

SOUTHWARK   STREET

WAHACA

BRITISH FILM
INSTITUTE

STREET

PARIS GARDEN

RENNIE STREET
COLOMBO STREET

BURRELL STREET

BEAR LANE
GREAT SUFFOLK STREET
CHANCEL

Holiday
Inn Express

SOUTHBANK
CENTRE

Hatfields
Green

DOON STREET
STAMFORD STREET

Waterloo & City line

CORNWALL ROAD

COIN STREET
AQUINAS STREET
THEED STREET

HATFIELDS

MEYMOTT STREET

Novotel

NICHOLSON STREET
SCORESBY STREET

Topolski
Century
Museum

ROUPELL ST

JOAN STREET

SOUTHWARK

WATERLOO
EAST

BELVEDERE

Waterloo
East Theatre

BRAD   STREET

Jubilee line

UNION   ST

GREAT SUFFOLK ST

YORK ROAD

Bakerloo line

Northern line

WATERLOO

MESON
DON FELIPE

THE
ANCHOR
& HOPE

NELSON

Nelson
Square

SURREY ROW

POCOCK STREET

BLACKFRIARS

RUSHWORTH STREET

CORNWALL RD
THE CUT
SHORT STREET

LAMBETH

STREET

UFFORD STREET

VALENTINE PLACE

WEBBER   STREET

WEBBER   STREET

LEAKE STREET

RADIO
DAYS

LOWER
MARSH
MARKET

Park
Plaza
County
Hall

LOWER MARSH

FRAZIER STREET

MARSH

ROAD

Hampton
by Hilton

GRAY STREET
BARON'S PLACE
WEBBER ROW

MILCOTE STREET
LANCASTER STREET
BOYFIELD STREET
SILEX STREET

SCOOTERCAFFÈ

BAYLIS

N

LAMBETH PALACE ROAD
UPPER MARSH

Tune
Hotel

LAMBETH
NORTH

ROYAL   STREET

PEARMAN STREET
MORLEY STREET
GERRIDGE STREET

DODSON STREET

ROAD

BOROUGH   ROAD

ROTARY STREET

WESTMINSTER BRIDGE RD

1.

SNOWDEN FLOOD

Unit 1.01 Oxo Tower Wharf,
Bargehouse Street, SE1 9PH
020 7401 8710,
snowdenflood.com
Mon–Fri 10.30am–6pm,
Sat 11am–6pm, Sun 12–5pm

For stylish holiday
mementoes, go no further
than Snowden Flood (so
named after its equally
stylish owner). Based in a
bijoux studio-meets-shop,
overlooking the Thames, there
are plates, cups, teapots and
coasters emblazoned with
gorgeous graphic London
skyline silhouettes (she
frequently designs for the
likes of the British Museum,
Chatsworth House and Tate
Modern). In the mix are retro
prints, featuring Art Deco
swimmers on washbags,
antique finds like silver milk
jugs or condiment sets, Kew
Gardens scented candles,
aprons and tea towels; and
most useful for the weary
traveller: Faust's Potions,
perfect for combating jetlag.
Snowden is one of the many
creatives based out of the first
and second floors of the Oxo
Tower so take the time to visit
these unique talents.

SOUTHBANK CENTRE

Belvedere Road, SE1 8XX
020 7960 4200,
southbankcentre.co.uk
Royal Festival Hall:
Mon–Sun 10am–11pm
Queen Elizabeth Hall, Hayward
Gallery and Purcell rooms:
closed for renovation, due to
re-open September 2017

Glean a sense of the pioneering spirit of British design at the Southbank Centre, created in 1951 for the Festival of Britain, and now encompassing the Royal Festival Hall, Queen Elizabeth Hall, Hayward Gallery and Purcell rooms. The Royal Festival Hall plays host to performances as diverse as book readings to philharmonic recitals. Grab something to eat or drink and enjoy the views from the outdoor terrace of the busy river life on the Thames. There's a daily second-hand book market and at weekends a thriving street food market. Underneath, its 'unofficial' graffitied skate space (the heart of London's skateboarding community for 40 years) helps lend this innovative arts institution a groovy edge.

3.

THE ANCHOR & HOPE

36 The Cut, SE1 8LP
020 7928 9898,
anchorandhopepub.co.uk
Mon 5–11pm, Tues–Sat 11am–
10.30pm, Sun 12.30–3.15pm

Perfectly placed between The Old and Young Vic theatres, this is a ramshackle, warm and welcoming pub where the artwork on the walls is for sale and dishes are generous and hearty. Operating on a first-come-first-served basis (put your name on the waiting list while enjoying a drink at the bar), or make new friends by joining a shared table. Emphasis is on British produce and seasonal flavours, a well-priced European wine list and great value three-course worker's lunch. Try the beef and barley bun with horseradish cream and fried potatoes; or any of the slow-cooked sharing dishes. But leave room for dessert – delights such as buttermilk pudding with blood oranges or muscat caramel custard aren't to be missed.

4.

SKYGARDEN

20 Fenchurch Street, EC3M 3BY
For access to the garden only
(free entry) 020 7337 2344,
for restaurants 0333 772 0020,
skygarden.london
Mon–Fri 10am–6pm, Sat–Sun
11am–9pm; bar & restaurants
Mon–Sun 7am–1am (with
unlimited access to the gardens)

For sweeping, uninterrupted views of London from a sky-high living garden, head over the bridge to Skygarden, in the top three floors of the 38-storey building dubbed locally as the Walkie Talkie. The garden is filled with agapanthus and bird of paradise, French lavender and rosemary. Entry is free but you have to book – make it easier and reserve a seat at the all-day **Darwin Brasserie**, treat yourself to lunch or dinner at the contemporary British **Fenchurch** or have a coffee in the **Sky Pod Bar**.

5.

THE FOUNDERS ARMS
52 Hopton Street, SE1 9JH
020 7928 1899,
foundersarms.co.uk
Sun–Thurs 9am–11pm, Fri–Sat
9am–12am

We always head here for a
lovely lazy Sunday lunch after
seeing the latest exhibition at
the Tate – if the spectacular
views across the river to
St Paul's and the city (and
all the to-ings and fro-ings
of barges, ferries and speed
boats on the Thames and
the trains rattling across
Blackfriars Bridge nearby)
isn't feast enough, there's the
very satisfying pub grub. Dine
on great sharing platters – the
Best of British boasts cheddar
and stilton cheeses, pork pies
and wild boar Scotch eggs;
prime beef burgers with
fat chips and slaw, healthy
goat's cheese salads with
quinoa and butternut squash,
all guaranteed to keep you
nourished when you head out
to explore.

6.

WAHACA

Queen Elizabeth Hall,
Southbank Centre,
Belvedere Road, SE1 8XX
020 7928 1876, wahaca.co.uk
Mon–Sat 12–11pm, Sun
12–10.30pm

Former British MasterChef
winner Thomasina Meirs
has combined her passion
for Mexican street food (the
memory of flavours and
spices from time spent living
and working there) with
the best seasonal and local
British ingredients. With
many outposts throughout
the city, this one is my
favourite for its flavours,
vividly coloured recycled
shipping containers, and
location with great views
of the Thames; the tequila
bar is a great spot to watch
the sunset. Healthy, hearty
dishes like messy, toasted
soft corn tortillas filled with
slow-cooked, Yucatecan-
marinated pork go well
with quesadillas filled with
long-cooked black beans
and Mexican herbs, and
doughnut churros with a
rich chocolate sauce team
with margaritas infused
with tamarind, hibiscus
or passionfruit.

7.

DANDELYAN

20 Upper Ground, SE1 9PD
020 3747 1000,
mondrianlondon.com
Mon–Thurs 4pm–1am, Fri–Sat
12pm–1.30am, Sun 12pm–
12.30am

It's been fascinating to
see the transformation of
the old Sea Containers
building (where I first
worked on arrival in London
as a marketing department
temp) into Ian Schrager's
new Mondrian hotel. British
designer Tom Dixon's
interiors evoke the mood of
a sexed-up, disco version of
the ballroom of an elegant
transatlantic Art Deco ocean
liner. Head to the Dandelyan
bar on the ground floor for a
signature cocktail by award-
winning mixologist Mr Lyan
(Ryan Chetiyawardana,
voted one of the city's key
movers and shakers by
London's well-respected
daily newspaper the *Evening
Standard*). Try a non-alcoholic
Dandelyan Sourless (apple
juice shaken with a floral
syrup, lime and egg white)
or for a little kick, a Catkin
mixed with Mr Lyan's gin,
blackberry, birch wine and
leaf, mint and caraway.

6.

7.

South Bank   129

There's loads to discover along the South Bank. Start at the **London Eye** (londoneye.com), the world's largest cantilevered observation wheel, which is now as much a London landmark as the nearby Houses of Parliament.

Book ahead to experience one of the stellar theatrical performances, starring the cream of Britain's acting talent, at the **National Theatre** (Upper Ground, SE1 9PX, nationaltheatre.org.uk). Ticket prices are generally affordable (especially at the Dorfman Theatre, which celebrates new writing).

Next door, the **British Film Institute**, aka BFI (Belvedere Road, SE1 8XT, bfi.org.uk) has a jam-packed program of new and old films, genre seasons and a Mediatheque library of over 2,500 films and TV programs you can watch for free (turn up or book ahead). Its London film festival in October boasts hundreds of films.

Take a detour through **Gabriel's Wharf** for quirky cafes and shops with a global beat, and the **Oxo Tower** for independent designers and makers.

No visit to London is complete without the **Tate Modern** (Bankside, SE1 9TG, tate.org.uk) – let the kids run up and down the immense Turbine Hall, browse the wonderful bookshop, and immerse yourself in contemporary exhibitions, celebrating everyone from Andy Warhol and Damien Hirst to Frida Kahlo.

Nearby, look for Ben Wilson's chewing gum art on the **Millennium Bridge**, grab a seasonal bite at **Albion** (NEO Bankside building, Holland Street) and discover affordable artworks at the **Bankside Gallery** (48 Hopton Street).

Designer–maker **Snowden Flood** opened her store in the Oxo Tower in 2010.

Lower Marsh Market

For weekday lunches (it's particularly good on a Friday), this market has an amazing range of international food, from Peruvian and Mexican to Thai and Vietnamese. On Saturdays, there's a small flea market.

Meson don Felipe (53 The Cut):

An oldie but a goodie tapas bar that's been here for years. There's a guitarist who climbs onto a teeny podium above the door to the toilets to serenade you while you eat and drink, instantly transporting you back to the Costa del Sol circa 1973.

Scootercaffè (132 Lower Marsh):

A very old favourite of mine that's a cafe by day and a bar with great cocktails by night. There's a nice terrace for sitting outside, or go downstairs to be surrounded by vintage scooter memorabilia. I also love their very nice cat.

Radio Days (87 Lower Marsh):

This is great for vintage clothes and memorabilia from the 1930s–70s, run by Lee, who has a very good eye.

Wagumi (Unit 1.08 Oxo Tower Wharf, Bargehouse Street):

A wonderful Japanese design and crafts shop with exquisite products.

East Mayfair takes you from the east side of the famous Bond Street through to the elegant stretch of Regent Street (one of the world's oldest and grandest shopping streets) bordered at the top by Oxford Circus and at the bottom by Piccadilly. Next door to the Royal Academy (*see* page 142) be seduced by the age-old charm of Burlington Arcade (*see* page 138).

Don't miss famed British shops such as fashion's doyenne of punk **Vivienne Westwood** (44 Conduit Street) and the Royal Warranted expert lingerie store **Rigby & Peller** (22A Conduit Street). For scent fanatics, **Jo Malone London**'s flagship store (101 Regent Street) is the spot to discover its exclusive Fragrance Library of discontinued and limited edition scents.

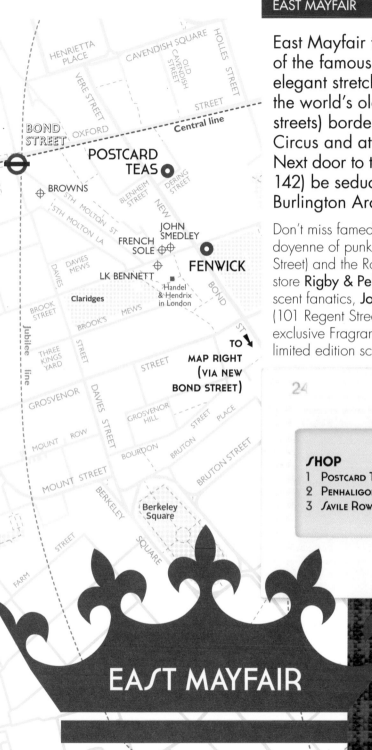

EAST MAYFAIR

TO
MAP RIGHT
(VIA NEW
BOND STREET)

ЅHOP
1 POSTCARD TEAS
2 PENHALIGONS
3 ЅAVILE ROW

ЅHOP AND EAT
BURLINGTON ARCADE
THOMAS'S AT BURBERRY
ЅHOP, EAT AND DRINK
BOND STREET
EAT AND DRINK
ЅKETCH

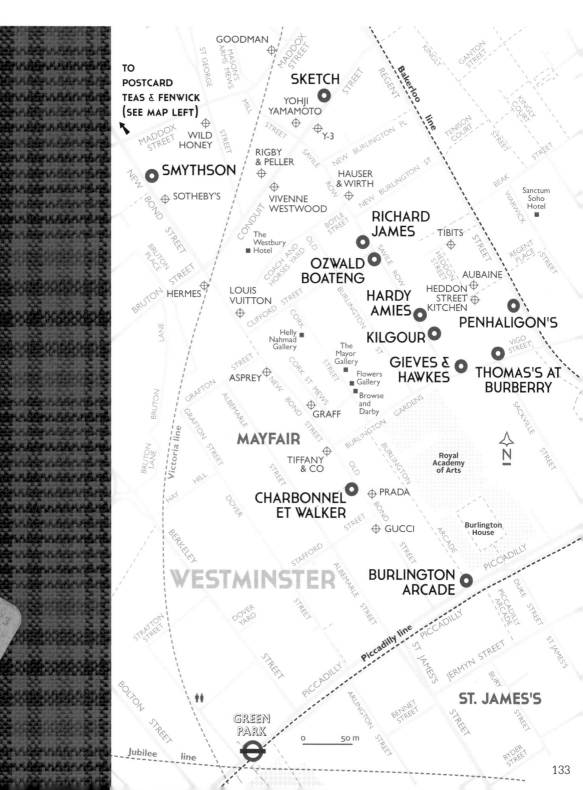

GOODMAN

ST GEORGE STREET

MASON'S ARMS MEWS

MADDOX STREET

**TO
POSTCARD
TEAS & FENWICK
(SEE MAP LEFT)**

SKETCH

YOHJI
YAMAMOTO

Y-3

MADDOX STREET

WILD
HONEY

MILL STREET

REGENT STREET

Bakerloo line

KINGLY STREET

GANTON STREET

KINGLY COURT

RIGBY
& PELLER

TENISON COURT

SMYTHSON

SOTHEBY'S

NEW BOND STREET

CONDUIT STREET

VIVENNE
WESTWOOD

HAUSER
& WIRTH

NEW BURLINGTON PL

NEW BURLINGTON ST

BEAK STREET

WARWICK STREET

Sanctum
Soho
Hotel

BRUTON STREET

BRUTON PLACE

HERMES

The
Westbury
Hotel

COACH AND HORSES YARD

OLD BURLINGTON STREET

BOYLE STREET

**RICHARD
JAMES**

SAVILE ROW

TIBITS

REGENT PLACE

LOUIS
VUITTON

**OZWALD
BOATENG**

**HARDY
AMIES**

HEDDON STREET

AUBAINE

PENHALIGON'S

LANE

CLIFFORD STREET

BURLINGTON STREET

CORK STREET

Helly
Nahmad
Gallery

The
Mayor
Gallery

KILGOUR

HEDDON
STREET
KITCHEN

VIGO STREET

STREET

ASPREY

NEW BOND STREET

CORK ST MEWS

Flowers
Gallery

Browse
and
Darby

**GIEVES &
HAWKES**

**THOMAS'S AT
BURBERRY**

SACKVILLE STREET

BRUTON LANE

GRAFTON STREET

GRAFF

BURLINGTON GARDENS

MAYFAIR

TIFFANY
& CO

OLD BOND STREET

BURLINGTON ARCADE

Royal
Academy
of Arts

N

HAY HILL

DOVER STREET

ALBEMARLE STREET

**CHARBONNEL
ET WALKER**

PRADA

GUCCI

Burlington
House

PICCADILLY

BERKELEY STREET

STAFFORD STREET

ALBEMARLE STREET

WESTMINSTER

**BURLINGTON
ARCADE**

PICCADILLY ARCADE

DUKE STREET

STRATTON STREET

DOVER YARD

DOVER STREET

Piccadilly line

PICCADILLY

ST JAMES'S STREET

JERMYN STREET

BURY STREET

ST JAMES'S

BOLTON STREET

ARLINGTON STREET

**GREEN
PARK**

0   50 m

BENNET STREET

ST. JAMES'S

RYDER STREET

Jubilee   line

133

1.

POSTCARD TEAS
9 Dering Street, W1S 1AG
020 7629 3654,
postcardteas.com
Mon–Sat 10.30am–6.30pm

Blink and you might miss this lovely slither of a shop off the Oxford Street end of Bond Street, with its beautifully curated teas from around the world. When Postcard Teas opened in 2008, the team were quick to give credit to the tea makers growing these most striking, pure teas by referencing their name and location on the beautifully illustrated caddies for all its 60 plus teas. They continue to support these family farms in China, Japan, Taiwan, Korea, and Vietnam. Try black, green, oolong, puerh and flavoured teas in the perfectly formed porcelain tea cups made by founder Tim d'Offay and ceramicist Peter Ting; and if you have time, arrange an individual tasting or join a Saturday morning tea masterclass.

2.
PENHALIGON'S

125 Regent Street, W1B 4HT
020 7434 2608,
penhaligons.com
Mon–Sat 10am–7pm, Thurs
10am–8pm, Sun 12–6pm

For many years, I've worked with a photographer whose Samson-esque mane of thick, silvery hair and subtle but secret woody citrus scent has made me go slightly wobbly at the knees. I finally worked out his fragrance was Penhaligon's Blenheim Bouquet. The Mayfair store is one of Penhaligon's most flamboyant stores in London, playing on the brand's Edwardian barbering roots and Beaux-Arts detailing of padded walls, jewel-hued ornate tiling and glass chandeliers. Here you'll find their 34 fragrances (all British-made), contained in glass bottles with ribbon-wrapped stoppers, including the founder William Penhaligon's first fragrance, Hammam Bouquet (inspired by the scent of a Turkish bath in 1872).

3.
SAVILE ROW

Between Conduit Street and Burlington Gardens you'll find the home and heart of British tailoring – through the windows you'll see artisans hard at work cutting, stitching and fitting. If you want something unique to take home, you can't beat a bespoke suit – **Gieves & Hawkes**, **Richard James** (photo 3B), **Ozwald Boateng** and **Kilgour** (photo 3C) are all here. For tighter purse strings, **Hardy Amies**'s legacy (photos this page and 3A) as a maverick menswear designer in the 1960s lives on at the revamped eponymous label, offering a sleek but accessible collection of men's separates and accessories. In Amies's words, 'a man should look as if he's bought his clothes with intelligence, put them on with care and then forgotten all about them.'

2.

3A.

3B.

3C.

2.

2.

BURLINGTON ARCADE
51 Piccadilly, W1J 0QJ
020 7493 1764,
burlington-arcade.co.uk

There is a wonderful old-world charm to the 19th century **Burlington Arcade**, originally built to house jewellers and watchmakers. With its curling wrought-iron gates and wood-panelled shopfronts, it will take you from Piccadilly up through to the back of the Royal Academy and on to Bond Street, passing by beautiful cashmere knits at **NPeal**, dainty macarons at **Laduree**, and heavenly heels by **Manolo Blahnik**. There are **Maison Michel** hats, witty bags, purses and clutches from **Lulu Guinness**, marvellous marquetry in picture frames, jewellery boxes and candles by **Linley** (the late Princess Margaret's son), monogrammed loafers at **Crockett & Jones**, and antique jewellery dealers **Richard Ogden** and **Michael Foster**. It's also home to fragrance specialists **True Grace**, **Frederick Malle** and **Roja Dove**. Just around the corner in Burlington Gardens is the recently relocated **Pickett**, with a cornucopia of rainbow-hued leather goods, jewellery, pashminas, gloves and keepsake boxes.

THOMAS'S AT BURBERRY

5 Vigo Street, W1S 3HA
020 3159 1410, burberry.com
Mon–Sat 8am–8pm,
Sun 11.30am–5pm

It doesn't get more British than a Burberry trench coat, and even if you can't afford the luxury label, enjoy a classic British breakfast of tea and hot buttered crumpets, or boiled egg and soldiers, in Burberry's all-day cafe called **Thomas's** (named after its innovative founder, who transformed the brand's fortunes with his invention of gabardine in 1870). The massive 44,000 square foot flagship store takes you through the brand's heritage from iconic outerwear to each season's catwalk collections, all designed by Christopher Bailey. It's a good spot for gifts – stationery, backgammon or bridge, Mohican bears and cashmere throws – or treat yourself to a monogrammed Burberry check scarf or a leather wallet embossed with your initials.

BOND STREET

Bond Street (and its New Bond Street extension, built just over a decade later in the 1720s) has long been the playground of the rich and famous. Alongside major luxury labels (**Gucci**, **Prada**, **Louis Vuitton**, **Hermès**, et al.), look for the Royal Warranted stationers **Smythson** (40 New Bond Street, photos this page top, 6B and C) and chocolatiers **Charbonnel et Walker** (28 Old Bond Street). At **Fenwick** department store (63 New Bond Street, photos 6A and D) I often whiz in for a quick peruse of its wonderful beauty hall and its eclectic yet elegant mix of designer and diffusion lines, stationery and kids gifts, and niche accessories from around the world. Turn onto Brook Street, passing knitwear master **John Smedley** and British shoe brands **LK Bennett** and **French Sole** along the way, until you reach South Molton Street and the trend-setting **Browns** fashion store. Spread over five inter-connecting townhouses, it has always championed the more unusual and daring designers, from Dries Van Noten to Alice Archer.

SKETCH

9 Conduit Street, W1S 2XG
020 7659 4500, sketch.london
Mon–Fri 8am–2am, Sat
10am–2am, Sun 10am–12am

Mourad Mazouz, in partnership with Michelin-starred chef Pierre Gagnaire, is always pushing the boundaries of taste, style and design with ever-evolving rooms, designed by contemporary artists, boasting a number of restaurants and bars within its three-storey location. **The Gallery**, open for afternoon tea and dinner (bookings recommended), serves sophisticated, pared back modern French dishes with an Asian twist. The room is the main attraction though, currently powdery pink by designer India Mahdavi, with walls (and tableware) decorated in sketches by artist David Shrigley. **Parlour** on the ground floor, and **The Glade** up one level are more casual, open for breakfast, light lunches and afternoon tea (I still dream of the tea sandwiches, made with bread so light and fluffy with fillings such as quail's egg and caviar); it's also the perfect place for a nightcap.

6A.

7.

6B.

6C.

7.

6D.

Off Regent Street, tucked away in the quiet of Heddon Street, you'll find casual, affordable eateries: organic veggie fare at **Tibits**, light French brasserie dishes at **Aubaine**, and modern British heartiness at Gordon Ramsay's **Heddon Street Kitchen**.

Along Piccadilly, the **Royal Academy of Arts** (Burlington House, Piccadilly, W1J 0BD, royalacademy.org.uk), founded in 1768, hosts major exhibitions (think Ai Wei Wei, David Hockney, Matisse and Anish Kapoor, et al.) as well as a summer exhibition, often its biggest drawcard. Here, any artist (famous, emerging or aspiring, from anywhere in the world) can submit work for exhibition. Make a beeline for the print room for limited editions by major artists at a fraction of the price. Its **Atelier Café**, at the rear on Burlington Gardens, is a perfect pit stop for coffee or a light lunch; its shop is fabulous for art books and exclusive designs in cards, scarves and jewellery by British artists.

For music fans, take a walk to **Handel's House** at 25 Brook Street, where he composed the famous *Messiah*, (being sure to pass **St George's** church (stgeorgeshanoversquare.org) on the way, the composer being its most famous parishioner). Coincidentally, **Jimi Hendrix** once lived next door at number 23, so both have recently been combined to form a museum (handelhendrix.org).

Dream of owning a Picasso or Warhol as you browse the eye-popping, museum-quality art up for auction at **Sotheby's** on Bond Street (also worth visiting for its chic little cafe). Best of all, everyone is welcome.

EAST MAYFAIR LOCAL RECOMMENDS

Jonathan Nunn was a Postcard Teas customer. Now he manages it.

Goodman

(24–26 Maddox Street): For serious steak, you can't beat Goodman's unusual cuts, dry-aged in-house, from corn-fed USDA or grass-fed British cows.

Fenwick

(*see* page 140): Its multiple restaurants offer a quiet respite from the bustle of Bond Street; and the range of cold-pressed juices and tonics from Botanic Lab on the ground floor (where co-founder and creative director Christophe Reissfelder has an excellent palate for flavour combinations) are always a notch above everyone else's.

Yohji Yamamoto/Y-3

(53–54 Conduit Street): Yohji Yamamoto is a hero of ours at Postcard Teas – I go more regularly to the Y-3 store directly opposite the mainline store for his diffusion line, a sportier take on classic Yohji silhouettes at a more affordable price.

Hauser & Wirth

(23 Savile Row): This huge space at the top of Savile Row houses Iwan and Manuela Wirth's London gallery, now one of the most important and influential in London for contemporary art. I always find it calming to come here on my lunch break, particularly when Pipilotti Rist once filled the whole gallery with beanbags to relax on while watching her video installations.

Wild Honey

(12 St George Street): Sister restaurant to Arbutus in Soho, the lunch deal for three courses is a steal considering the location, Michelin-star cooking and the beautiful wood-panelled dining room.

Map labels

BELLAMY'S
DRAKES
BOURDON STREET
BRUTON
RUPERT SANDERSON
Helly Nahmad Gallery
BRUTON STREET
CLIFFORD STREET
TIMOTHY EVEREST
BRUTON PL
BARLOW PLACE
BRUTON LANE
CORK STREET

TO MAP RIGHT (VIA BERKELEY SQUARE & MOUNT STREET)

NEW BOND STREET
ALBEMARLE STREET
Victoria line
Berkeley Square
ANNABEL'S
SEXY FISH
DOVER STREET
PAUL SMITH
NOBU
FITZMAURICE PLACE
CHARLES ST
CLARGES MEWS
BERKELEY STREET
STRATTON STREET
STREET
STREET
CURZON STREET
BOLTON STREET
The Washington Mayfair
CLARGES STREET
GREEN PARK
YE GRAPES
Jubilee line
Hilton London Green Park
KITTY FISHERS
Flemings Mayfair
WHITE HORSE ST
PICCADILLY
Piccadilly line
Green Park

WEST MAYFAIR

SHOP
1 THE NEW CRAFTSMEN
2 PAUL SMITH
3 MOUNT STREET
4 RUPERT SANDERSON

24   JUN 8016

17

EAT AND DRINK
CLARIDGE'S

West Mayfair, stretching west of Bond Street towards Park Lane, topped by Marble Arch and bottomed by Hyde Park Corner, is largely residential with its rows of elegant red-bricked Georgian houses intermingling with grand hotels and swanky shops.

Take time to sit in **Berkeley Square** under the shade of its very tall plane trees, some of the oldest in central London. Around here, it's an unusual mix of world-class art galleries (**Phillips**, **Gagosian**), a Rolls Royce dealership and discreet members-only clubs (including the famous **Annabel's**, favourite of the aristocracy). For a moment's peace, escape into Royal Warranted **H.R. Higgins** on Duke Street for a great cup of tea or coffee and cake.

THE NEW
CRAFTSMEN

H.R. HIGGINS

THE COLONY
GRILL ROOM AT
THE BEAUMONT

CLARIDGE'S

BROWN HART
GARDENS

GEORGE YARD

London
Marriott
Hotel

TAYLOR
STREET
BARISTAS

MAYFAIR

Franklin
Roosevelt
Memorial

September 11
Memorial
Garden

HEDONISM
WINES

Dwight
D. Eisenhower
statue

Grosvenor
Square
Gardens

Ronald
Regan
statue

ROLAND
MOURET

NICHOLAS
KIRKWOOD

0   50 m

THE
CONNAUGHT

ROKSANDA
ILINCIC

CHRISTIAN
LOUBOUTIN

SCOTT'S

GOYARD

→

TO
RUPERT
SANDERSON
& PAUL SMITH
(SEE MAP
LEFT)

MARC JACOBS

CREED

SIMONE
ROCHA

MOUNT
STREET
GARDENS

Grosvenor
Chapel

WESTMINSTER

Hyde
Park

The Dorchester

1.

THE NEW CRAFTSMEN

34 North Row, W1K 6DG
020 7148 3190,
thenewcraftsmen.com
Mon–Sat 10am–6pm

For centuries, old Blighty was world-renowned for its artisan crafts but over time these have become increasingly lost. Design industry veterans Mark Henderson, Natalie Melton and Catherine Lock launched The New Craftsmen in 2012 to bring contemporary British craftsmanship to a new audience. In their light and airy showroom, just off the Marble Arch end of Oxford Street, there are hand-thrown, paper thin ceramics by Stuart Carey, sensually carved knotty wooden spoons and bowls by Nic Webb and quirkily hand-block-printed cushions by Laura Loakes. These sit alongside willow woven trays and traditional scissors forged in Yorkshire, jewel-coloured glass, and Scottish spun and knitted throws.

PAUL SMITH
9 Albemarle Street, W1S 4BL
020 7493 4565,
paulsmith.co.uk
Mon–Wed 10am–6pm, Thurs–
Sat 10am–7pm, Sun 12–6pm

Fashion designer (Sir) Paul
Smith is a British treasure
– adored for his slim-line,
tailored suits in unexpected
colours; his signature multi-
coloured stripe pattern,
used on jacket linings, rugs
and teapots; and his quirky
and eclectic style. The
store mirrors Paul Smith's
clothing ethos – 'upper-class
tailoring brought together
with something silly', and
features tables supported
by giant scorpions, books
about Eduardo Paolozzi,
porcelain plates with ponies
by Seletti, sculptural clothing
rails, wood-block floors, walls
of dominos or lined with
Paul's drawings, and vintage
furniture covered in a suiting
or shirting fabric. The cast-
iron panelled facade, with an
elliptical motif of interlocking
circles (which inspired the
No. 9 collection of bags and
wallets), stands out in this
Regency street.

3.
MOUNT STREET

For a calming escape from the frenetic shopping of Oxford, Regent and Bond streets, wander around old Mayfair – being sure to look up through the windows to see amazing painted ceilings and chandeliers that mark the area's magnificent Georgian history. Wind your way up through Berkeley Square and on to Mount Street, where there is a growing community of British designers – **Roksanda Ilincic** (number 9, photos 3A and D), **Nicholas Kirkwood** (number 5), **Simone Rocha** (number 93) and **Roland Mouret** (8 Carlos Place). You can also window shop at **Goyard, Marc Jacobs**, **Christian Louboutin** and **Creed**. Stop to admire the Tadao Ando 'water sculpture' outside **The Connaught** (photos this page top and 3B) then head inside to revel in elegant splendour with a Fleurissimo Champagne cocktail (first created for Princess Grace of Monaco) in the **Connaught Bar** or retreat to the cosseting warmth of the **Coburg Bar** for the best club sandwich and homemade crisps (it's pricey but deliciously worth it). Opposite is the relatively secret (but open to the public) **Mount Street Gardens** (photo 3C) where you can sit with a coffee and book, and breathe in the fresh garden air. Another great British institution is **Scott's** (number 20, photos this page bottom, 3E and F) – sit at the bar with a glass of crisp Muscadet and octopus carpaccio and enjoy a spot of people-watching.

3A.

3B.

3C.

3D.

3E.

3F.

4.

RUPERT SANDERSON

19 Bruton Place, W1J 6LZ
020 7491 2260,
rupertsanderson.com
Mon–Fri 10am–6.30pm,
Sat 11am–6.30pm

Not too many cobblers name designs after British daffodils – names like Little Gem and Moonara, Flare and Hera – but Rupert Sanderson is known for doing the unexpected, like ditching a career in advertising for a shoe-making course at Cordwainers College, then working for Sergio Rossi and Bruno Magli before setting up on his own in 2001. Cate Blanchett, Naomi Watts and Nicole Kidman are all fans, and collaborations include working with fashion designers Karl Lagerfeld and Antonio Berardi. Flattering, leg-lengthening metallic heels, military-detailed boots, and pointy-toed suede flats (packaged in avocado-green boxes, the colour inspired by his mother's placemats) play not to catwalk fads but represent the high quality leathers and tools of his trade. They may slightly blow the budget but they're worth the investment for years to come.

5.

CLARIDGE'S

Brook Street, W1K 4HR
020 7629 8860,
claridges.co.uk
Mon–Sun 12pm–1am

I love nothing more than sinking into one of **The Fumoir Bar**'s aubergine velvet banquettes at Claridge's – it's possibly the most glamorous bar in possibly the most glamorous hotel in London. As William Klein's iconic 1958 'Smoke and Veil' portrait of Evelyn Tripp stares down from above the 1929 brushed steel and Lalique crystal bar, the time of day disappears in this darkened, intimate space, especially over a signature Flapper cocktail (fresh strawberries and Champagne, invented when the bar opened). The never-ending courtesy nibbles alone make it worth a visit. The **Foyer & Reading Room** is *the* place to enjoy afternoon tea in London (bookings essential), with rare teas, sumptuous sandwiches and intricate patisserie fripperies, whilst immersed in Claridge's famed Art Deco detailing and signature *eau de nil* green and white hues (from carpets to tea services).

Rupert Sanderso

151

It's pure joy to wander around the streets of west Mayfair, taking in the exquisite 18th century architecture of the area's elegant townhouses where many of the city's great and good have lived over the years. Once I spied a house on Chesterfield Street boasting a double blue plaque; it had been home to both the former British prime minister Anthony Eden and (although not at the same time) 18th century dandy George 'Beau' Brummell (friend of the Prince Regent, then the future King George IV).

At **Hyde Park Corner**, pay homage to heroes from days gone by at the Australian and New Zealand war memorials. Climb the magnificent **Wellington Arch**, featuring a sculpture of the Angel of Peace descending on a four-horsed chariot of war, which was originally built as the north gate to Buckingham Palace. At the top, take in panoramic views of west London and nearby leafy Hyde and Green parks. Also visit **Apsley House** (english-heritage.org.uk), Wellington's splendid Georgian home.

For major glamour, don't miss **Sexy Fish** (pop in just to see the amazing art works and murals by architect Frank Gehry and artist Damien Hirst) and **Nobu Berkeley** (Berkeley Square). Cocktails and chicken pot pie in **The Colony Grill Room** at **The Beaumont** is always fun (Brown Hart Gardens). In **Shepherd Market**, check out affordable, stylish menswear at **Simon Carter**, leather goods at **Tanner Krolle**, the handsome, eccentric pub **Ye Grapes** or pop in to see new and arthouse flicks at the **Curzon Cinema**.

Shoe designer **Rupert Sanderson** opened his store in 2003.

Timothy Everest (35 Bruton Place): The place I go to for my favourite navy linen suits (there's also a more affordable, casual collection of ready-to-wear tailoring for those not looking for made-to-measure).

Taylor Street Baristas (22 Brooks Mews): For my morning coffee on the way to work. They make the best macchiato (featuring the house Rogue Espresso roasted blend of beans) in town.

Bellamy's (18/18A Bruton Place): This is my home from home, where I love to order the salad of artichoke heart and haricots verts (apparently it's the only restaurant the Queen dines at).

Hedonism Wines (3–7 Davies Street): A great place to discover something new from a sommelier-sourced collection of thousands of wines from around the world.

Kitty Fishers (10 Shepherd Market): This is a crazy, small modern British restaurant, hidden away in Shepherd Market with a fantastic chef and great vibe.

Drakes (3 Clifford Street): A great spot for the finest ties, handmade in London, from specialist Italian and British woven cloths.

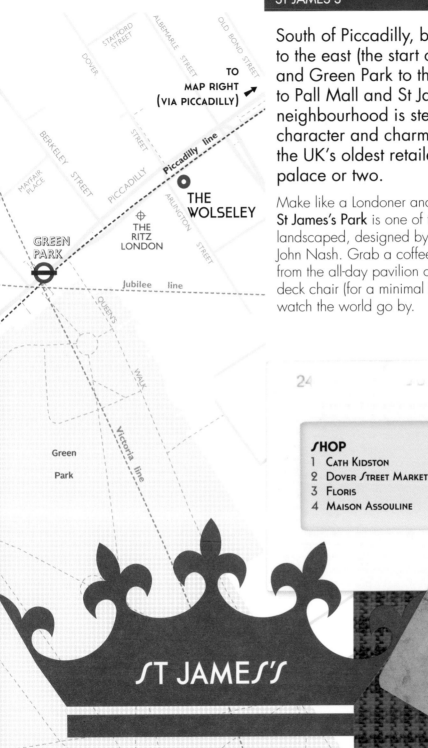

ST JAMES'S

South of Piccadilly, between Haymarket to the east (the start of the theatre district) and Green Park to the west, and down to Pall Mall and St James's Park, this neighbourhood is steeped in historical character and charm, including some of the UK's oldest retailers and just a royal palace or two.

Make like a Londoner and relax in a royal park – **St James's Park** is one of the most beautifully landscaped, designed by the Regency architect John Nash. Grab a coffee and something to eat from the all-day pavilion cafe **Inn The Park**, hire a deck chair (for a minimal fee per hour) and happily watch the world go by.

SHOP
1 CATH KIDSTON
2 DOVER STREET MARKET
3 FLORIS
4 MAISON ASSOULINE

SHOP, EAT AND DRINK
FORTNUM & MASON
EAT AND DRINK
THE WOLSELEY
DRINK
DUKES BAR

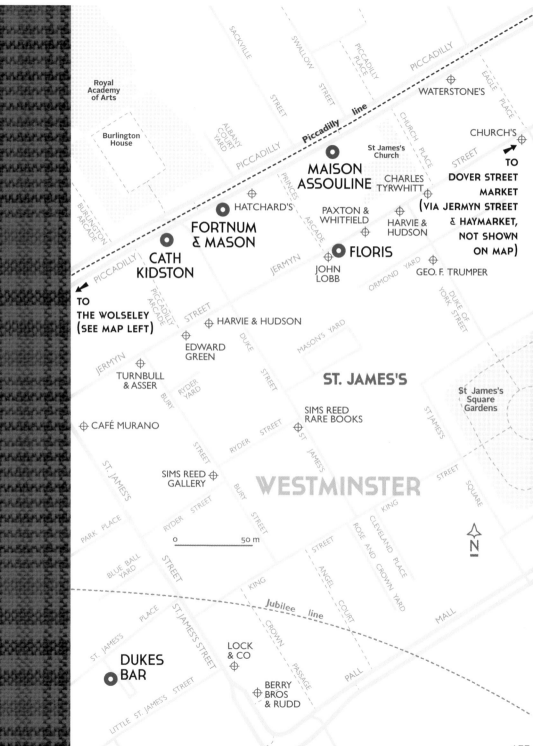

Royal Academy of Arts

Burlington House

St James's Church

WATERSTONE'S

CHURCH'S

TO DOVER STREET MARKET (VIA JERMYN STREET & HAYMARKET, NOT SHOWN ON MAP)

Piccadilly line

MAISON ASSOULINE

CHARLES TYRWHITT

PAXTON & WHITFIELD

HATCHARD'S

FORTNUM & MASON

HARVIE & HUDSON

CATH KIDSTON

FLORIS

JOHN LOBB

GEO. F. TRUMPER

TO THE WOLSELEY (SEE MAP LEFT)

HARVIE & HUDSON

EDWARD GREEN

ST. JAMES'S

St James's Square Gardens

TURNBULL & ASSER

SIMS REED RARE BOOKS

CAFÉ MURANO

SIMS REED GALLERY

WESTMINSTER

0   50 m

N

Jubilee line

DUKES BAR

LOCK & CO

BERRY BROS & RUDD

1.

CATH KIDSTON

178–180 Piccadilly, W1J 9ER
020 7499 9895,
cathkidston.com
Mon–Sat 10am–8pm,
Sun 12–6pm

Cath Kidston creates practical, everyday useful things that make you smile. She started designing in 1993 with a Rose Bouquet print – since then, her beautiful, very English designs have blossomed into a multi-million dollar empire with stores worldwide. Her flagship store still maintains the charm of those first days when Cath was making cushion covers and bags from vintage fabric finds. Her 'modern vintage' patterns of re-scaled and re-coloured roses, flowers, British birds, spots, retro cowboys and nostalgic city scenes can be found on everything from backpacks to bed sheets, coats to cushions, wallpaper to wallets. A perfect (and affordable) memento from your London visit.

2.

DOVER STREET MARKET

18–22 Haymarket, SW1Y 4DG
020 7518 0680,
doverstreetmarket.com
Mon–Sat 11am–7pm,
Sun 11am–5pm

Dover Street Market (so-named after its original location where Victoria Beckham has now set up shop, at number 36) has relocated to Haymarket, in what was once Burberry's HQ, near to the Theatre Royal and Haymarket Hotel. It was pioneered by Comme des Garçon's Rei Kawakubo and husband Adrian Joffe, whose designs feature prominently throughout the market. Much like Colette in Paris and Milan's 10 Corso Como, the team behind this multi-floor, multi-brand edgy alternative to the traditional department store, hunts down new, exciting and often daring fashion, fragrance and gadgets. Here you'll find big fashion names, rising stars, DSM's own collaborations, select homewares and an outpost of Paris's Rose Bakery.

3.

FLORIS

89 Jermyn Street, SW1Y 6JH
020 7747 3612,
florislondon.com
Mon–Wed & Fri 9.30am–
6.30pm, Thurs 9.30am–7pm,
Sat 10am–7pm, Sun 11.30am–
5.30pm

It's fragrance paradise at
Royal Warranted Floris, the
oldest British fragrance
house – ninth-generation
owned and based in the same
spot that its Menorcan barber
and comb-maker founder
Juan Famenias Floris set
up in 1730. It's still the hub
where all their fragrances
are developed (production
is in Devon). Come here for
elegantly curated scents –
infused with classic notes like
rose, lily of the valley, leather,
amber, lime, sandalwood
and lavender – available
in fragrances, scented
candles, triple-milled soaps,
room sprays and body
products; plus wonderful
accessories, like smart
Briar wood and gold-plated
shaving kits, soap bowls and
luxurious beard oils for men,
goosedown powder puffs and
handcreams for women.

4.

MAISON ASSOULINE

196A Piccadilly, W1J 9EY
020 3327 9370, assouline.com
Mon–Sat 10am–8pm, Sun
11am–6pm

Prosper and Martine
Assouline made their names
publishing glossy coffee
table books with substance
20 years ago when they self-
published a book about one
of their favourite hotels, La
Colombe d'Or, in the south
of France. They still follow
their nose for adventure and
publish books focusing on
style and glamour: fashion
designers, shoes, supercars,
racing yachts, jewels, elegant
hotels, and Michelin-starred
chefs. Maison Assouline
brings together its founders'
passion for the good things
in life, all under one roof.
Here you'll find an on-site
traditional bookbinder and
you can enjoy a Side Car or
espresso at the Maison's
Swans Bar.

3.

4.

4.

3.

3.

4.

5.

FORTNUM & MASON

181 Piccadilly, W1A 1ER
020 7734 8040,
fortnumandmason.com
Mon–Sat 10am–8pm, Sun
11.30am–6pm

Fortnum & Mason encapsulates the nostalgia of a bygone era when British elegance and refinement reigned. First opened in 1707 as a grocer, it supplied the palace with specialty goodies from around the world and even supplied famous explorers with provisions for expeditions. Today, Fortnum's is most famous for its beautifully packaged chocolates, biscuits, teas and jams, and amazing window displays. Don't miss the glamorous beauty floor with exclusive lotions and potions and neatly edited selections of fashion and home accessories, stationery and tableware. Pop into **Parlour** for coffee (served with a tiny cone of gelati) and an overflowing ice-cream sundae, just what kids' dreams are made of; or visit the **Diamond Jubilee Tea Salon** for rare teas, fresh-baked scones with lemon curd or jam and clotted cream. Discover a new aged old-world or sprightly new-world wine with a plate of Fortnum's own gently cured smoked salmon, in the lower-ground **Wine Bar**.

6.

THE WOLSELEY

160 Piccadilly, W1J 9EB
020 7499 6996,
thewolseley.com
Mon–Fri 7am–12am, Sat
8am–12am, Sun 8am–11pm

Just the thrill of the elegant Art Deco surroundings makes The Wolseley an ultimate London experience. Previoulsy the Wolseley Motors showroom in the 1920s, with its Venetian and Florentine influences in the towering pillars and geometric-patterned marble floors, today it's the perfect backdrop to Chris Corbin and Jeremy King's signature brasserie fare. From Viennese-inspired warming bowls of chicken soup with dumplings and generous schnitzel to black forest gateau and apple strudel. It bustles all day, so drop in for breakfast or morning coffee and pastries; for lunch, afternoon cocktails and late night suppers it's best to book in advance.

James's

7.

DUKES BAR
Dukes Hotel, 35 St James's
Place, SW1A 1NY
020 7491 4840, dukeshotel.com
Mon–Sat 2–11pm,
Sun 4–10.30pm

I have it on good authority from my martini friends that this is THE place to have a martini in London. It's said author Ian Fleming took inspiration from a Dukes martini for James Bond's preference for 'shaken not stirred'. Tucked away down a cobbled lane off St James's Street, Dukes Bar is an intimate, old-fashioned affair but worth the crush for the art of what legendary bartender Alessandro Palazzi takes very seriously. A trolley is wheeled over to your table, where a glass is spritzed with the mere hint of vermouth from what looks like an elegant perfume atomiser; from there on, the rest is tailor-made according to your tastes.

Jermyn Street has long been a discerning gentleman's paradise. Here you'll find smart shirt-makers **Charles Tyrwhitt** and **Turnbull & Asser**; traditionally made shoes at **Church's** and **John Lobb**; suits for all budgets, from affordable at **Harvie & Hudson** to debonair; and at British grooming institution **Geo. F. Trumper** (1 Duke of York Street), you can pop in for a quick haircut, beard trim or hot-towel wet shave. At **Paxton & Whitfield** (93 Jermyn Street), one of the city's best cheesemongers, try a bit of special reserve Wensleydale or Lincolnshire Poacher (there's great cheese accessories to take home too).

For an over-the-top afternoon tea experience, book in advance for the gilded Palm Court at **The Ritz** on Piccadilly (remember jacket and tie is essential, and strictly no trainers).

Along Piccadilly, bibliophiles should look out for the flagship stores of the six-level **Waterstone's** and five-level **Hatchard's** (London's oldest bookshop, open since 1797, and booksellers to the Royal Households).

Both **Buckingham Palace** and the Prince of Wales' home **Clarence House** are essential visits for their sumptuous interiors, amazing art and interesting tidbits about Royal life. Book ahead to avoid disappointment, go early to avoid the crowds and don't miss the gift shops (see royalcollection.org.uk). In summer, at the end of the Buckingham Palace tour, it's glorious to sit on the terrace with an ice-cream and appreciate the beauty of the garden.

In stark contrast, the **Institute of Contemporary Art** (aka ICA, ica.org.uk) celebrates only the most radical art and culture with exhibitions, talks and film showings.

Simon Thompson is restaurant director for 45 Jermyn Street.

Lock & Co (6 St James's Street): This St James's institution has been around since the 1600s – not only the oldest hat shop in the world, it's also the oldest family-run business still in existence. Oscar Wilde and Beau Brummel were huge fans.

Edward Green (75 Jermyn Street): Quintessentially English shoe-makers from Northampton where you can have a pair custom-made or choose from their beautiful selection. They also do a lovely scarf.

Fortnum & Mason Food Hall (*see* page 160): The ultimate place to source some really special produce for a dinner at home. I like to pop in for their parmesan, smoked salmon and Glenarm beef.

Café Murano (33 St James's Street): Angela Hartnett's Michelin-starred Italian-inspired cooking (just like her Grandma used to make) never disappoints.

Sims Reed Gallery & Rare Book Shop (43A Duke Street): Their collection of first editions and rare books is amazing, their photographic and art reference books always make great gifts.

Alfred Dunhill (48 Jermyn Street): I head here for tailored suits and silk ties.

Berry Bros & Rudd (3 St James's Street): With over 300 years' experience in the world of wine and as suppliers to the palace since King George III, BBR knows all about the fruits of the vine (it offers wine tastings and dinners held in its atmospheric cellars, too).

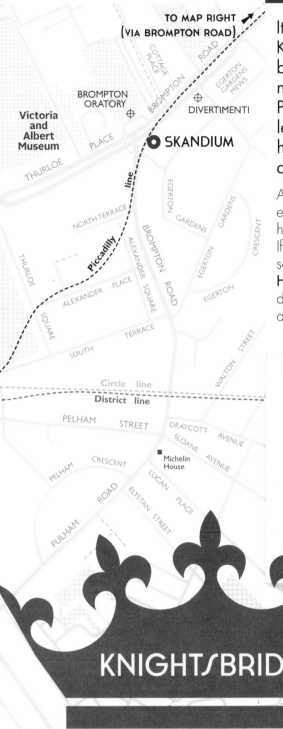

TO MAP RIGHT
(VIA BROMPTON ROAD)

It doesn't come any ritzier than Knightsbridge, with billionaire boys driving fast cars around the neighbourhood, views of leafy Hyde Park, luxury fashion brands lining the length of Sloane Street, and of course, it's home to two of the world's most exclusive department stores.

At **Harrods** explore the food hall, bursting with exotic and luxurious delicacies; the clothes, handbags and homewares are pretty fabulous too. If you want a memento, one of the iconic Harrod's souvenir bears or bags will fit nicely in a suitcase. **Harvey Nichols'** window displays are always a delight, and it's a veritable heaven for fashionistas and gourmands.

24   JUN 8016

SHOP
1 ANYA HINDMARCH BESPOKE
2 CUTLER AND GROSS
3 RACHEL VOSPER
4 SKANDIUM

17

SHOP, EAT AND DRINK
PRET-A-PORTEA AT
THE BERKLEY
EAT AND DRINK
BAR BOULUD

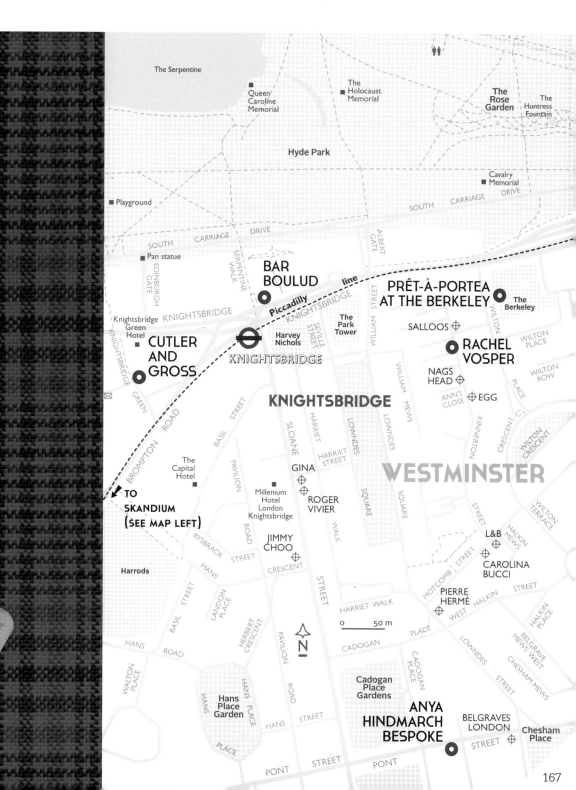

The Serpentine

Queen Caroline Memorial

The Holocaust Memorial

The Rose Garden

The Huntress Fountain

Hyde Park

Cavalry Memorial

SOUTH CARRIAGE DRIVE

Playground

SOUTH CARRIAGE DRIVE

ALBERT GATE

Pan statue

EDINBURGH GATE

SERPENTINE WALK

BAR BOULUD

Piccadilly line

KNIGHTSBRIDGE

Knightsbridge

WILTON STREET

PRÊT-À-PORTEA AT THE BERKELEY

The Berkeley

WILTON PLACE

Knightsbridge Green Hotel

CUTLER AND GROSS

Harvey Nichols

SEVILLE STREET

The Park Tower

SALLOOS ✦

WILTON ROW

KNIGHTSBRIDGE GREEN

KNIGHTSBRIDGE

RACHEL VOSPER

WILLIAM MEWS

NAGS HEAD ✦

WILTON PLACE

BROMPTON ROAD

BASIL STREET

SLOANE STREET

HARRIET STREET

LOWNDES STREET

ANN'S CLOSE ✦ EGG

WILTON CRESCENT

KNIGHTSBRIDGE

KINNERTON STREET

WILTON CRESCENT

The Capital Hotel

PAVILION ROAD

Millenium Hotel London Knightsbridge

GINA

ROGER VIVIER

LOWNDES SQUARE

CADOGAN SQUARE

WESTMINSTER

WILTON TERRACE

TO SKANDIUM (SEE MAP LEFT)

RYSBRACK STREET

HANS STREET

JIMMY CHOO

WALTON STREET

L&B

MOTCOMB STREET

HALKIN MEWS

CAROLINA BUCCI

HALKIN STREET

Harrods

CRESCENT

PIERRE HERMÉ

WEST HALKIN STREET

HALKIN PLACE

HARRIET WALK

0   50 m

PLACE

LOWNDES STREET

BELGRAVE MEWS WEST

HANS ROAD

LANDON PLACE

HERBERT CRESCENT

PAVILION ROAD

CADOGAN

N

CHESHAM MEWS

HANS PLACE

PAVILION ROAD

Cadogan Place Gardens

CADOGAN PLACE

CHESHAM STREET

WALTON PLACE

BASIL STREET

Hans Place Garden

HANS PLACE

HANS STREET

ANYA HINDMARCH BESPOKE

BELGRAVES LONDON

STREET

Chesham Place

PLACE

PONT STREET

PONT STREET

167

1.

ANYA HINDMARCH BESPOKE

15–17 Pont Street, SW1X 9EH
020 7838 9177,
anyahindmarch.com
Mon–Sat 10am–6pm

Anya Hindmarch started in the handbag business at just age 19, with the idea of a rucksack she'd spotted on her gap year in Italy. Today, she's transformed how we think about our handbags, teaming brilliant organisation (labelled internal pockets or individual carry cases for everything you can think of), with irreverent fun – recent designs have imitated cornflake packets and men at work signs. At this store, customisation is king – a handwritten message or a child's doodle can be embossed onto everything from the inside of a bag to luggage tags and jewellery cases by artisans instore. A favourite motto can grace the cover of your diary, a keepsake box can be inlaid with a photograph; there's a made-to-measure wallet service too. These are heirlooms in the making.

2.
CUTLER AND GROSS
16 Knightsbridge Green,
SW1X 7QL
020 7581 2250,
cutlerandgross.com
Mon–Sat 9.30am–7pm,
Sun 12–5pm

For over 40 years, founders
Graham Cutler and Tony
Gross have been creating
high quality, hand-finished,
elegantly streamlined (no
logo, no bling) frames, made
in Italy and adored by the
fashion industry (Erdem,
Giles Deacon and Victoria
Beckham are just a few of
their co-collaborators) and
red carpet regulars like
Rihanna and Sir Elton John.
At the Piers-Gough designed
Knightsbridge store, there's
also a permanent archive
display of over 4,000 frames
dating back to the brand's
inception in 1969, and a
service where you can design
your own dream pair of specs
which they'll then get made
for you.

3.
RACHEL VOSPER
69 Kinnerton Street, SW1X 8ED
020 7235 9666,
rachelvosper.com
Mon–Wed & Fri–Sat 10am–
6pm, Thurs 10am–7pm

Leading candle chandler
Rachel Vosper's tucked-
away boutique has a warm,
welcoming rustic feel with its
floorboards, antique display
cabinets and flea market
objets d'art. Here, Rachel
works her waxy magic
with natural formulations,
designed to allow for a longer
and more even burn, in
scents such as invigorating
echinacea and rich, full-
bodied spiced amber, smoky
French lavender or elegant
rose and neroli. You can
buy them ready-poured, in
lovely tactile round-bottom
glass vessels, or there's a
bespoke service for filling
anything from teacups to
gigantic Murano vases.
Book to join a candle making
course (held one Saturday
every month).

4.

SKANDIUM
245–249 Brompton Road,
SW3 2EP
020 7584 2066, skandium.com
Mon–Wed & Fri–Sat 10am–
6.30pm, Thurs 10am–7pm,
Sun 11am–5pm

In 1999 a Swede, Finn and
Dane (Magnus Englund,
Christina Schmidt and
Christopher Seidenfaden
respectively) decided
to Scandi-fy the UK by
opening Skandium, first in
Marylebone and then with
this large two-floor furniture
and accessories space. Here,
alongside the classic Arne
Jacobsen for Fritz Hansen egg
chairs and Eames loungers,
Skandium has the very best of
Northern European designers
showcasing Scandinavian
modernism with brands
like Stelton, Vitra, Georg
Jensen, Marimekko, Hay
and Rosendahl. There's
everything from teapots,
soaps, bowls, throws, garlic
presses, candlesticks and
trays, to bedside clocks. Don't
miss the collector's editions
of Moomintroll ceramics
and Klaus Haapaniemi's
folkloric designed tableware
too. But my favourite pick?
The Oiva Toikka glass birds
for Iittala.

5.

PRÊT-À-PORTEA AT THE BERKELEY
Wilton Place, SW1X 7RL
020 7235 6000,
the-berkeley.co.uk
Mon–Thurs 1.45–5.30pm,
Fri–Sun 1–5.30pm

For the ultimate London fashion and food experience, go no further than the delightfully witty, good fun Prêt-à-Portea afternoon tea in the **Collins Room** at The Berkeley. A genius brainwave by the hotel group's Publicity Director Paula Fitzherbert, I was lucky enough to spend a few afternoons taste-testing sweet treats whilst drinking Champagne (oh, life can be tough!) before it officially launched. Food treats are inspired by catwalk collections, so expect Manolo Blahnik or Jimmy Choo biscuit heels, Valentino studded fondant sponge handbags, Matthew Williamson macarons, and Dolce & Gabbana bavarois pannacottas. Tea in harlequin-patterned Wedgwood china, tea sandwiches, taster spoons and savoury skewers add to the delight. Booking ahead is essential.

6.

BAR BOULUD

Mandarin Oriental Hyde Park,
66 Knightsbridge, SW1X 7LA
020 7201 3899, barboulud.com
Mon–Sat 12pm–1am,
Sun 12pm–12am

This secret little gem, tucked underneath the Mandarin Oriental in the heart of Knightsbridge, serves up dreamy comfort food that's surprisingly affordable for such five-star hotel opulence (booking not essential; a seat at the bar is always fun). Sister restaurant to star chef Daniel Boulud's Bar Boulud in NY, this is a great place for a delicious shared plate of specialty sausages (including boudins blanc and noir), traditional rillettes and patés infused with cognac or truffle, or a perfectly formed burger filled with melt-in-the-mouth slow-cooked meats. The pièce de résistance however is the little cloth-wrapped parcel of hot-from-the-oven madeleines at the end of the meal – with a glass or two of rosé.

Along Brompton Road, don't miss British fashion leather label **Mulberry**, and kitchen emporium and cook school **Divertimenti**.

Down Sloane Street, find luxe shoe designers **Gina**, **Jimmy Choo** and **Roger Vivier**, and timeless ladylike fashion by **Emilia Wickstead**, one of the Duchess of Cambridge's favourites. Over on Motcomb Street, seek out modernist gold woven friendship bracelets and delicate hoop earrings by fourth-generation Florentine jeweller **Carolina Bucci**, the softest monogrammed bedlinen at **L&B**, and chocolate treats at **Pierre Hermé** (13 Lowndes Street).

Hyde Park, created in 1536 as Henry VIII's hunting playground, sprawls across 350 acres of parklands and rose gardens with the **Serpentine** lake at its heart.

It hosts fantastic summer pop concerts and a Christmas Winter Wonderland. Throughout the park, statues pay homage to war heroes, the Holocaust and Queen Caroline (the wife of King George II who created the Serpentine and the Long Water in Kensington Gardens). Hire a row boat or pedalo, take a swim in the **Lido**, grab a coffee from the **Lido Bar and Cafe** or dip your toes in the **Diana Princess of Wales Memorial Fountain**.

The Serpentine Gallery, showcasing diverse and divisive contemporary art, commissions leading architects each summer to design a temporary pavilion for everyone to enjoy. Nearby, the **Sackler Gallery** (in a former 1805 gunpowder store) is attached to **The Magazine**, a modern restaurant extension designed by Zaha Hadid, serving modern European food for breakfast, brunch, afternoon tea and dinner.

Candle connoisseur **Rachel Vosper** opened her store in 2011.

Koffmann's (The Berkeley, Wilton Place): The croquettes d'escargots are fabulous, as are the staff. Something good always seems to happen when I'm here – like stumbling across the location for my first store.

Salloos (62–64 Kinnerton Street): The most vibrant and fresh Pakistani food you'll find anywhere in London, owned and run by the same wonderful family for 40 years. Try the pulao jahengiri for comfort or the chicken jalfezi if you're feeling brave.

Egg (36 Kinnerton Street): Maureen Doherty, founder of Egg, is retail royalty and her visual merchandising is awe-inspiring. Shop for classic cottons and linens you'll wear and love forever (she also did all the staff uniforms at Skye Gyngell's Spring restaurant).

Pandora (16–22 Cheval Place): Bursting with second-hand designer and vintage clothes, handbags and shoes, I recently purchased an exquisite Erdem dress here for a song.

Belgraves London (20 Chesham Place): This hotel's bar and terrace (with whiskey and cigar tastings) are perfect for unwinding in the early evening. Interior designer Tara Bernerd's home-from-home environment is also perfect. Sophie Michell's excellent menu in the **Pont St Restaurant** (Clarence Court boiled eggs with sourdough soldiers, superfood salads, venison cottage pie or rhubarb meringue pie) should also be sampled.

Nags Head (53 Kinnerton Street): The ultimate intimate drinking establishment. No mobile phones tolerated. The live jazz on the first Sunday of each month is legendary. Have a Guinness next to the fire and soak up the fascinating memorabilia.

Chelsea is a glamorous pocket of London, with designer shopping and chi-chi restaurants and bars to match. It was once the hot spot for daring artistic expression, first the bohemian Pre-Raphaelite Victorian artists and then home to punk (where Vivienne Westwood and Malcolm McLaren's Sex shop was located at Worlds End).

King's Road's two miles of shopping starts at Sloane Square with **Peter Jones** (part of the UK's best loved department store John Lewis) and takes in **Duke of York Square**'s mix of fashion and eateries, heads down past **Chelsea Town Hall** (a regular spot for arts and crafts fairs), and ending at **Worlds End**, so named after the pub built there in 1897.

DESIGNERS GUILD

GREEN & STONE

THE SHOP AT BLUEBIRD

CABBAGES & ROSES

THE BUILDER'S ARMS

ANTHROPOLOGIE

HABITAT

CHELSEA TOWN HALL

TO MAP RIGHT (VIA KING'S ROAD)

St Luke's Gardens

ALBERT BRIDGE

River Thames

BATTERSEA BRIDGE

CHELSEA

ƎHOP
1 ANTHROPOLOGIE
2 DESIGNERS GUILD
3 LIZ EARLE
4 MONICA VINADER
5 THE WHITE COMPANY

24   JUN 8076

17

SHOP **AND** EAT
DAYLESFORD ORGANIC
Elizabeth Street
SHOP, EAT **AND** DRINK
The Shop at Bluebird
EAT
CAFÉ PRESTAT
CHELSEA PHYSIC GARDEN

CADOGAN
PLACE
CADOGAN
SQUARE
Cadogan
Place
Gardens
CLABON
CADOGAN
PAVILION
SLOANE
LYALL
STREET
EATON
SQUARE
CHESTER SQUARE
Cadogan
Square
Gardens
SLOANE
EATON
PLACE
EATON
ELIZABETH
STREET
CHESTER SQUARE
MEWS
MOORE STREET
SQUARE
CADOGAN PL
BELGRAVIA
CADOGAN
HALL
EATON
EATON
SQUARE
St. Michael's
**ELIZABETH
STREET** ⊙
ROAD
STREET
CLIVEDEN
PLACE
EATON
SOUTH
CHESTER ROW
EATON
TERRACE
Circle line
District lines
THE
BOTANIST
DAVID
MELLOR
⊕ COLBERT
CAROLINE
TERRACE
EATON
PLACE
CAFÉ PRESTAT
**THE WHITE
COMPANY**
THE ROYAL COURT THEATRE
🚻 ⊖ 🚻 **SLOANE SQUARE**
ANNOUSHKA ⊕
DRAYCOTT
PLACE
PETER
JONES
LIZ EARLE
CUISINE DE BAR
BY POILÂNE
**MONICA
VINADER**
HOLBEIN
EBURY
STREET
**DAYLESFORD
ORGANIC**
🚻
ST
BOURNE
SLOANE GARDENS
St Barnabas
ROAD
JOHN
SANDOE
BOOKS
KING'S
CHELTENHAM TERRACE
SAATCHI
GALLERY
PLACE
PIMLICO
BLOOMFIELD
TERRACE
✉
**TO
ANTHROPOLOGIE,
THE SHOP AT
BLUEBIRD &
DESIGNERS GUILD
(SEE MAP LEFT)**
WALPOLE STREET
FRANKLIN'S
TURKS ROW
ROW
Burton
Court
HOSPITAL
CHELSEA BRIDGE ROAD
CHELSEA
0   100 m
EBURY BRIDGE ROAD
⬆ N
Chelsea
Synagogue
ORMONDE GATE
EAST ROAD
Royal
Hospital
Chelsea
ROYAL
Ranelagh
Gardens
CHRISTCHURCH STREET
ROYAL HOSPITAL ROAD
WEST
ROAD
National
Army
Museum
Royal
Hospital
Grounds
**CHELSEA
PHYSIC
GARDEN**
TITE
STREET
🚻 ⊙
EMBANKMENT
GARDENS
TANGERINE
DREAM
CAFÉ
SWAN WALK
DILKE STREET
**CHELSEA
EMBANKMENT**
⊕
Thames
River

179

1.

ANTHROPOLOGIE

131–141 King's Road,
SW3 4PW
020 7349 3110,
anthropologie.com
Mon–Sat 10am–7pm,
Sun 12–6pm

American lifestyle and fashion
emporium Anthropologie
oozes with a colourful,
patterned, embellished,
vintagey and handcrafted
feel. Everything from floaty
dresses, bright knits,
patterned tablecloths and
napkins, to witty plates and
eclectic necklaces, is at its
best in this cavernous space,
situated in the lovingly
restored former Antiquarius
antiques arcade (with a
fabulous decorative Art
Nouveau tiled facade). It's
a veritable treasure trove
of pieces gathered from all
around the world by a buying
team always on the go.
Here you're certain to find
something beautiful to take
home. Don't miss its small
separate gallery at the front,
hosting evolving exhibitions
by British and international
artisans and artists.

DESIGNERS GUILD

267–277 King's Road,
SW3 5EN
020 7351 5775,
designersguild.com
Mon–Sat 10am–6pm,
Sun 12–5pm

Designers Guild is a British design institution, founded in the 1970s by the ever-glamorous Tricia Guild, whose signature floral prints feel 'contemporary, not sentimental' (as she describes them) in their bold, painterly, rich and vivid hues, worked across bedding, cushions, wallpaper, soft furnishings and upholstery. Instore, Tricia teams her own designs with favourite finds from her travels, whether it's a newly-graduated potter or an intricate gold necklace by a favourite jeweller. Easy things to pack in the suitcase include generous-sized napkins, kids' bedding, sculptural ceramics by artist Kate McBride, fluoro notebooks, washbags, prettily packaged scented candles and soaps, chopping boards and paint-splattered bowls. All with Designer Guild's distinctive technicolour kick.

3.

LIZ EARLE

38–39 Duke of York Square,
SW3 4LY
020 7881 7750, uk.lizearle.com
Mon & Wed–Sat 10am–7pm,
Tues 10.30am–7pm, Sun
11am–5pm

Walking into British skincare brand Liz Earle's flagship store feels like being submerged in a soothing pale blue sea, surrounded by the store's driftwood-inspired natural materials and colours. Liz Earle's naturally active formulations are packaged in understated containers (all recyclable of course), with the delicious blend of scents like orange flower, rose, neroli, lavender and rosemary in the air. The Hot Cleanse & Polish cleanser apparently sells every 30 seconds somewhere in the world. This is the place for affordable, gentle botanical-inspired skin, bath and body products, beauty and health advice (there are treatment rooms too, or ask for a hand and arm massage while you browse).

4.

MONICA VINADER

71–72 Duke of York Square,
SW3 4LY
020 7259 9170,
monicavinader.com
Mon–Wed & Fri–Sat
10am–7pm, Thurs 10am–8pm,
Sun 11.30am–6pm

A-list favourite Monica Vinader's passion for creating candy-coloured rings, pendants and earrings has infused each of her collections since launching in 2006, with an ethos of dramatic, organic shapes at affordable prices. Here you'll find semi-precious stones (like moonstone, quartz, onyx, labradorite, amethyst and aquamarine), hand-cut and faceted in contemporary shapes for bold cocktail rings and earrings; pendants in stones, patterned from ancient coins, and initials, bought individually or grouped together on a long necklace, lend a talismanic effect. Monica's woven and metal friendship bracelets make the perfect gift (for yourself or others).

4.

4.

3.

4.

4.

3.

5.

THE WHITE COMPANY

4 Symons Street, SW3 2TJ
020 8166 0199,
thewhitecompany.com
Mon–Sat 10am–7pm,
Sun 11.30am–5.30pm

It was former magazine stylist Chrissie Rucker's passion for all things white that originally inspired the launch of her mail-order catalogue in 1994, selling a neatly edited selection of quality bedding and lifestyle accessories that fit perfectly with the minimalist design mood of the time. Now with a booming empire of stores UK-wide, here, in her first ever store, is still the best place to see all The White Company has to offer: signature white mixed with muted hues of grey, camel and navy in delicately embroidered or hemstitched Egyptian cotton bedding, fluffy towels and luxury loungewear for stylish loafing. There's a sleek capsule collection of everyday fashion separates, home fragrances, tableware and even nightwear and bedlinen for kids.

6.

DAYLESFORD ORGANIC

44B Pimlico Road, SW1W 8LP
020 7881 8060,
daylesford.com
Shop: Mon–Sat 8am–8pm,
Sun 10am–4pm; cafe: Mon–Sat
8am–7pm, Sun 10am–3pm

All things organic and biodynamic don't come much chic-er than at Daylesford – a heavenly temple to healthy living, sustainable farming and exquisite, minimalist packaging. Founder Carole Bamford aims to serve the very best that her family's Cotswold's farm (and the producers around it) can grow, bake and bottle. This urban farmshop and cafe also boasts a butcher, bakery, grocer, and the cafe emphasises a seasonal menu of raw slaws and salads – expect lots of nuts, seeds, avocado and kale – and warming treats like Welsh rarebit or poached eggs on fresh-baked toasted sourdough. There are products for home, body and bath and the family's own wine label is on sale – its Château de Léoube rosé is one of the best.

ELIZABETH STREET

Elizabeth Street in Pimlico is a lovely stretch of shops and places to eat. For scent aficionados, **Jo Loves** (photo 7C) is the latest venture by Jo Malone – complete with a 'Fragrance Brasserie Bar', designed to enhance your experience of her bath and body scents, creams, cleansers and colognes; and **Les Senteurs** (photo 7D), London's oldest perfumery, carrying over 350 scents created by some of the world's best 'noses'. Find once-in-a-lifetime dream hats at **Philip Treacy**, a favourite of Lady Gaga and Sarah Jessica Parker. Grab a flaky pastry and strong coffee at **Baker & Spice** or an elaborately decorated sweet treat from **Peggy Porschen Cakes** (116 Ebury Street). There's good pub grub (chilli salt squid, beer battered fish and chips) at **Thomas Cubitt** (photos 7A and B), Sardinian-inspired pizzas and pasta at **Oliveto** or grab a glass of something intriguing (a Bordeaux-style Croatian red perhaps?) with a lamb burger at local favourite **The Ebury Restaurant and Wine Bar** (139 Ebury Street).

THE SHOP AT BLUEBIRD

350 King's Road, SW3 5UU
020 7351 3873,
theshopatbluebird.com
Mon–Sat 10am–7pm,
Sun 12–6pm

The Shop at Bluebird is a heavenly place to linger – across 10,000 square feet of exposed pipework and tiled floors in what was a garage originally built for the Bluebird Motor Company in 1923. A modern vibe comes with neon signs and handbags on pedestals alongside an ever-evolving unusual and exciting array of independent rising fashion stars to big names – some good value, some pricey – next to the owners' own label Jigsaw. Niche skincare and fragrance brands mix with design curiosities such as witty homewares by Fornasetti and David Downton's fashion illustration gallery. If you're feeling peckish, downstairs there's a cafe (complete with gin garden), bakery and gourmet grocer; upstairs, head to the bar for an 'experimental' fizz and modern Euro dishes like Goan monkfish curry or creamy chicken pie.

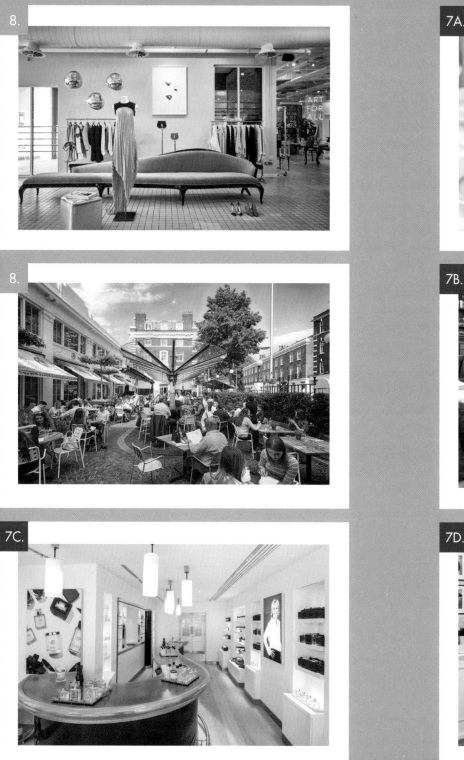

ART
FOR
ALL

CAFÉ PRESTAT

186 Pavilion Road, SW3 2BF
020 7730 7715, prestat.co.uk
Mon–Sat 8am–6.30pm,
Sun 9am–6pm

There's a 'spiffy and jolly good show' Britishness to the Royal Warranted chocolate makers Prestat and its bright pink, red, green and royal blue boxed chocs (with pretty illustrations by artist Kitty Arden). Run by brothers Bill Keeling and Nick Crean, Prestat was first started in 1902 by descendants of Louis Dufour (credited with creating the world's first chocolate truffle in Chambery, France). With its mix of rich marc de Champagne, gin and tonic, or red velvet truffles (made famous in Roald Dahl's book *My Uncle Oswald*), salted caramel thins and artisan Florentines, posh chocolate spreads and tins of hot chocolate, this little cafe is ideal for a quick slice of homemade cake, breakfast bowl of granola or lunchtime quiche.

10.

CHELSEA PHYSIC GARDEN

66 Royal Hospital Road,
SW3 4HS
020 7352 5646,
chelseaphysicgarden.co.uk
Garden only: Mon–Sun
10am–dusk, November–March;
garden and cafe: Tues–Fri & Sun
11am–6pm, April–October

London's green landscape is enviable for such a large, bustling city, and nothing beats escaping into Chelsea Physic Garden: a teaching and apothecary garden founded in 1673, boasting a unique living collection of over 5,000 edible, medicinal and historical plants and more than 100 different types of rare and endangered trees. During summer come for lunch over a glass of homemade lemonade or ginger beer at the garden's **Tangerine Dream Café**, attached to the Curator's House (access subject to an entry fee). It boasts vivid, seasonal British and Mediterranean flavours – goat's cheese tarts, fresh salads of pulses and beans, duck confit, with sumptuous cakes (orange polenta, coffee and walnut) or lavender scones for dessert.

Around Sloane Square, **The Botanist** and **Colbert** jostle, humming with a busy vibe, from breakfast to nightcaps. Don't miss a gander in **David Mellor**, famous for Sheffield steel cutlery and beautiful kitchen accessories. In the evening, **Cadogan Hall** (5 Sloane Terrace, SW1X, cadoganhall.com) offers a wonderful, intimate setting for author talks, and classical, contemporary and jazz concerts.

Saatchi Gallery (Duke of York's HQ, King's Road, SW3 4RY, saatchigallery.com) is a hot spot for fashion exhibitions for big brands like Chanel and Hermès, as well as showcasing founder Charles Saatchi's collection of daring, irreverent contemporary artists (he was one of the first to invest in works by Damien Hirst, Sarah Lucas and Gary Hume). The light, airy cafe, overlooking

playing fields, is a perfect spot for coffee and cake.

Halfway down King's Road, be inspired by the art supplies at **Green & Stone** and the affordable contemporary homewares at **Habitat** (founded by Sir Terence Conran in the 1960s). Take a detour to Sydney Street for gardening kit at **The Chelsea Gardener** and beautiful linens at **Cabbages & Roses**. Nearby, find charming old pubs with a modern gastro bent like **The Admiral Codrington** (17 Mossop Street) and **The Builder's Arms** (13 Britten Street).

If there's time, potter through Chelsea's elegant streets down to the **Chelsea Embankment**, lined with quiet little garden enclaves to sit in, and views across the ornate Albert Bridge to **Battersea Park** (and its famous Peace Pagoda) on the other side of the Thames.

CHELSEA LOCAL RECOMMENDS

The White Company's founder **Chrissie Rucker** opened her first store on Sloane Square in 2001.

The Royal Court Theatre
(Sloane Square): This wonderful not-for-profit drama company is highly respected for its contributions to modern theatre. Book Monday night tickets for £10, for a seat anywhere in the house.

John Sandoe Books (10 Blacklands Terrace): An independent bookshop since 1957, crammed with thousands of fiction, non-fiction and classic titles.

The Little Black Gallery (13A Park Walk): I go here to satisfy my love for black and white fashion photography.

Cuisine de Bar by Poilâne
(39 Cadogan Gardens): An outpost of the famous French bakery, this is a great place to meet friends for breakfast over fresh-baked breads and pastries or light tartines, made to order, at lunchtime.

Annoushka (41 Cadogan
Gardens): My good friend Annoushka Ducas showcases intricate, feminine modern collections featuring precious and semi-precious stones, and a curated mix of emerging and established guest designers.

South Kensington, located south of Hyde Park and west of Knightsbridge, is famous for its museums – the Victoria & Albert Museum, Science Museum and Natural History Museum – but it's also a buzzing precinct of shops, cafes and restaurants, with elegant Georgian garden squares and impressive mansions.

Around the Tube station, on Cromwell Place and Old Brompton Road, there's a variety of good value, casual eateries if you're feeling museum fatigue. But before you leave, don't forget to admire the magnificent neo-classical beauty of the nearby **Brompton Oratory**.

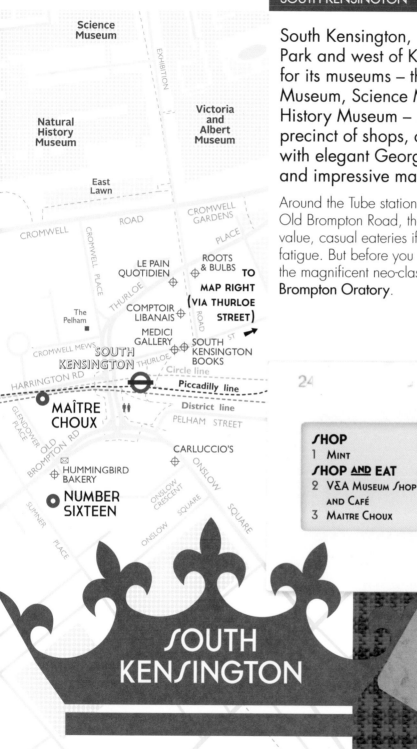

SHOP
1 MINT
SHOP AND EAT
2 V&A MUSEUM *SHOP* AND CAFÉ
3 MAITRE CHOUX

SHOP, EAT AND DRINK
THE CONRAN *SHOP*
EAT AND DRINK
TOM'S KITCHEN
NUMBER *SIXTEEN*

SOUTH KEN/INGTON

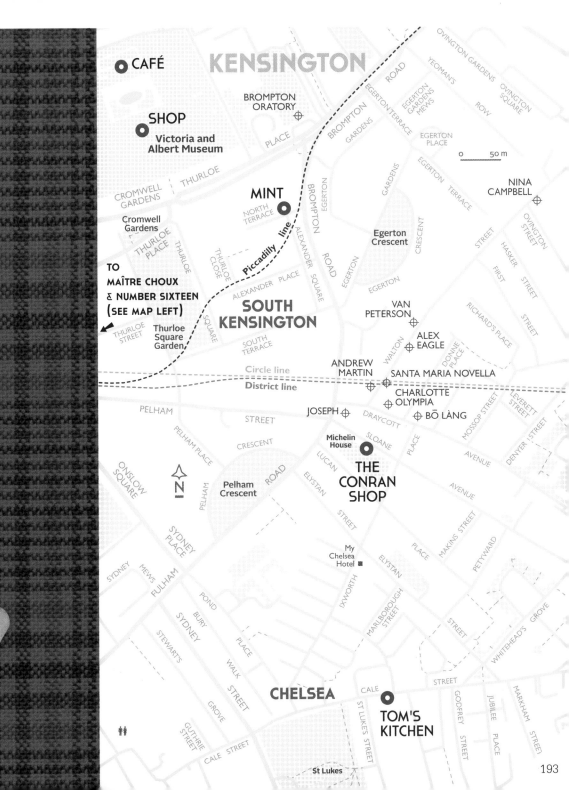

KENSINGTON

● CAFÉ

BROMPTON
ORATORY

● SHOP
Victoria and
Albert Museum

CROMWELL
GARDENS

THURLOE

● MINT
NORTH
TERRACE

Cromwell
Gardens

THURLOE
PLACE

THURLOE
CLOSE

Piccadilly line

NINA
CAMPBELL

0   50 m

Egerton
Crescent

EGERTON TERRACE

OVINGTON GARDENS

YEOMAN'S
ROW

OVINGTON
SQUARE

BROMPTON
ROAD

BROMPTON
GARDENS

EGERTON TERRACE

EGERTON GARDENS MEWS

EGERTON
PLACE

EGERTON
TERRACE

OVINGTON
STREET

HASKER
STREET

FIRST
STREET

RICHARD'S PLACE

ALEXANDER
SQUARE

ALEXANDER PLACE

TO
MAÎTRE CHOUX
& NUMBER SIXTEEN
(SEE MAP LEFT)

THURLOE
STREET

Thurloe
Square
Garden

SOUTH
KENSINGTON

SOUTH
TERRACE

VAN
PETERSON

ALEX
EAGLE

WALTON

DONNE
PLACE

ANDREW
MARTIN

SANTA MARIA NOVELLA

CHARLOTTE
OLYMPIA

Circle line

District line

PELHAM

STREET

JOSEPH

DRAYCOTT

BŌ LÀNG

MOSSOP STREET

DENYER STREET

LEVERETT
STREET

PELHAM PLACE

CRESCENT

Michelin
House

SLOANE

ONSLOW
SQUARE

PELHAM
Crescent

PELHAM ROAD

LUCAN
STREET

ELYSTAN
STREET

THE
CONRAN
SHOP

PLACE

AVENUE

AVENUE

MAKINS STREET

PETYWARD

N

SYDNEY
PLACE

My
Chelsea
Hotel ■

ELYSTAN

ELYSTAN
STREET

SYDNEY
MEWS

FULHAM

POND
PLACE

BURY
WALK

IXWORTH

MARLBOROUGH
STREET

STREET

WHITEHEAD'S GROVE

SYDNEY
STREET

STEWARTS

GROVE

CALE

CHELSEA

● TOM'S
KITCHEN

GODFREY
STREET

JUBILEE
PLACE

MARKHAM
STREET

GUTHRIE
STREET

CALE STREET

ST LUKE'S STREET

St Lukes

♿

193

1

MINT

2 North Terrace, Alexander
Square, SW3 2BA
0207 225 2228,
mintshop.co.uk
Mon–Wed & Fri–Sat 10.30am–
6.30pm, Thurs 10.30am–
7.30pm

Under Lina Kanafani's keen
curatorial guidance, Mint
mixes up cutting edge design
by emerging talent, one-off
and limited edition pieces
commissioned exclusively
for the store, and exhibitions
of thought-provoking work
by major design stars from
around the world. There
are chairs constructed from
leather, kilim rugs, lace-
imprinted concrete platters,
woven wicker cabinets and
steel drinks trolleys with a
Deco feel. It's the perfect
place for gleaning a little
inspiration from intriguing
designers experimenting
in unusual materials like
jesmonite, salvaged lagoon
timbers, rag rugs, cork and
bamboo basket weaving.
Mint is always a highlight
during the London Design
Festival in September.

2

V&A MUSEUM SHOP AND CAFÉ

Cromwell Road, SW7 2RL
020 7942 2000, vam.ac.uk,
vandashop.com
Shop: Mon–Thurs 10am–
5.30pm, Fri 10am–9.45pm;
café: Sat–Thurs 10am–5.15pm,
Fri 10am–9.30pm

I often do a fly-by visit to the
V&A just for its shop and
café. Whether you're after
gorgeous art coffee table
books, stationery, classy
London souvenirs or gifts for
the hard-to-buy, this place
has it. There are cabinets
of delightful jewellery and
exclusive limited edition
prints by British artists. The
V&A café is set in three
rooms – the original Morris,
Gamble and Poynter rooms –
decorated with exquisite
tiles, richly patterned
wallpaper and original 19th
century details; the classic
British fare – from tasty filled
rolls to fresh, seasonal salads,
plus great coffee and cake –
make this a worthwhile
destination in its own right.

3.

MAÎTRE CHOUX

15 Harrington Road, SW7 3ES
020 3583 4561,
maitrechoux.com
Mon–Fri 8am–8pm, Sat–Sun
10am–7pm

First it was cupcakes, then macarons, doughnuts and now eclairs – and Maître Choux's are the prettiest and fanciest you dare ever imagine. Slender couture-worthy eclairs, light choux profiteroles and *chouquettes* (pearl sugar-crusted little buns) are baked fresh every morning by three Michelin-star, Biarritz-born pastry chef Joakim Prat – and filled with light, luscious flavoured creams, from caramelised banana and intense chocolate to raspberry mousse, then glazed and decorated (with popcorn, roasted pecans, matcha tea) to dazzle the eyes as much as the tastebuds. There are a few seats instore where you can sit and enjoy these sweet treats, teamed with a cup of hot chocolate inspired by a Basque recipe from Joakim's grandmother, or you can take-away.

MAÎTRE
CHOUX

ARTISTE PATISSIER

4

THE CONRAN SHOP

Michelin House,
81 Fulham Road, SW3 6RD
020 7589 7401,
conranshop.co.uk
Mon–Tues & Fri 10am–6pm,
Wed–Thurs 10am–7pm, Sat
10am–6.30pm, Sun 12–6pm

Sir Terence Conran opened The Conran Shop in 1987, in what was once the British headquarters for the Michelin Tyre Company – the Art Deco facade still features the original tile work and inside is an array of beautiful mosaic scenes. Now under the direction of son Jasper, a world-leading fashion and homewares designer in his own right, it's a one-stop destination for furniture, homewares, kitchen kit, tableware, gifts and toys, with pieces designed by various members of the Conran empire or sourced from artisans and independent designers around the world. In the entrance, stop for a pint of prawns and the best baguette in town at the oyster bar, buy some succulent seafood to take-away from the Crustacea Stall in the covered forecourt, or enjoy a quick coffee amongst the florist's flowers.

TOM'S KITCHEN

27 Cale Street, SW3 3QP
020 7349 0202,
tomskitchen.co.uk
Mon–Fri, 8am–11.30am,
12–2.30pm & 6–10.30pm, Sat
10am–3.30pm & 6–10.30pm,
Sun 10am–3.30pm & 6–9.30pm

Tom Aikens may well have been one of the UK's youngest chefs to earn a Michelin star at age 26 – having trained under culinary greats Pierre Koffmann and Joel Robuchon – but what he does best is straightforward, simple British pub fare. Sourcing from UK suppliers – fresh fish and seafood from Cornwall, succulent beef from the Lake District, and organic veg from a worker's co-operative in the Lea Valley – it's hard to resist his seven-hour lamb confit or burger with triple-cooked chips. This is a great spot for brunch, alongside the full English breakfast, signature dishes include brioche French toast with caramelised apples or ham hock and mustard hash brown, topped with a poached egg and mustard sauce.

6.

NUMBER SIXTEEN

16 Sumner Place, SW7 3EG
020 7589 5232, firmdale.com
Mon–Sun 3–5.30pm

Set in a row of Victorian
stucco terraced houses that
have been transformed into
a boutique hotel, Number
Sixteen is another gem in Kit
Kemp's Firmdale hotel group,
filled with her distinctive
mix of vibrant interiors and
unusual art. The garden is a
well-kept secret and the most
blissful place to sit, especially
in summer, while devouring
scones with clotted cream
and strawberries dipped
in chocolate. I love taking
friends for afternoon tea after
a saunter around the nearby
museums – its secluded quiet
always surprises them. You
needn't be a guest to visit
but booking ahead is a good
idea. For those watching
waistlines, there's also a novel
fruit-themed afternoon tea –
various skewers and salads
made up of fresh berries
and exotic fruits – and tea
from My Cup of Tea includes
blends like Halmari Assam
and Silver Needle.

Around South Ken's Tube station there are tartines at **Le Pain Quotidien**, raw foodie delights at **Roots & Bulbs**, and good Italian fare at **Carluccio's**; head to **Hummingbird Bakery** for decadent cupcakes. I never miss the wonderful **South Kensington Books** and the impressive cards and stationery at the **Medici Gallery** next door.

Walton Street has great homewares at **Andrew Martin** and **Nina Campbell**, fragrance at **Santa Maria Novella**, fashion at **Alex Eagle** and jewellery at **Van Peterson**; on Draycott Avenue don't miss **Charlotte Olympia**'s witty, colourful shoes and bags.

South Kensington's trio of remarkable museums are all free (excepting some temporary exhibitions). The **Victoria & Albert Museum** (corner Cromwell and Exhibition roads, vam.ac.uk) celebrates contemporary and historical art and design across fashion, jewellery, textiles, ceramics, sculpture and furniture. On a sunny day, sit with tea and cake by the reflecting pond in the museum's central John Madejski Garden. Opposite the V&A is the **Natural History Museum** (nhm.ac.uk), known as the 'Dinosaur Museum' by London's youngsters, with giant skeleton bones of dinosaurs and whales. But there's much more to explore, from how insects communicate to what a meteorite looks like. The **Science Museum** (sciencemuseum.org.uk), also on Exhibition Road, inspires all the senses. From astronomy and cosmology to physics, chemistry, navigation and time, the aim here is to better understand the world (and universe). All have great shops (the Science Museum especially so for intriguing, inspiring kids' gifts) and the Natural History Museum is a fab spot for ice-skating at Christmas.

Lina Kanafani opened Mint in 1998.

Victoria & Albert Museum (*see* page 194): This wonderful place provides me with a never-ending source of inspiration and ideas.

Comptoir Libanais (1–5 Exhibition Road): For a little rest, pop into this lively, colourful Lebanese chain to quench your thirst with a homemade lemonade (with hints of rose or apple, mint and ginger), share a plate of hot and cold mezze (dips, olives, mana'esh flat breads), rest your feet, and watch life go by!

Joseph (77 Fulham Road): I occasionally like to indulge here in the latest luxuries. This multi-brand store stocks all the most desirable fashion labels, like Azzedine Alaïa, Chloé, Alexander Wang, Isabel Marant, Peter Piloto, and The Row, as well as its own upmarket collections.

Bō Làng (100 Draycott Avenue): Following a good browse of the shop, there is some of the best dim-sum to be found in London at this trendy restaurant where dumplings, buns and rolls come steamed or baked, alongside bowls of stir-fried noodles.

Think Notting Hill, think Portobello Road – antique dealers, food and street stalls and yes, *that* famous blue door on Westbourne Park Road, now sadly painted over. Home to the famous Notting Hill Carnival every summer, it still oozes with the bohemian spirit that once made the area so famous.

Although now largely home to bankers and A-listers, with property prices to match, the pretty sugar-almond-hued Georgian terrace houses, tree-lined streets and great shopping make it endlessly appealing. Westbourne Grove and Ledbury Road boast cool fashion and homewares, and don't miss **The Electric Cinema**, a Notting Hill institution for watching the latest films with a glass of wine in plush surrounds.

THE CROSS
SUMMERILL & BISHOP
COWSHED

St Johns

MELT CHOCOLATES

HOLLAND PARK

Central line

Norland Square

TO
MAP RIGHT
(VIA HOLLAND PARK AVENUE & PEMBRIDGE ROAD)

24   JUN 8016

SHOP
1 COUVERTURE & THE GARBSTORE
2 COWSHED
3 THE CROSS
4 LEDBURY ROAD

17

SHOP CONTINUED
HONEY JAM
LUTYENS & RUBINSTEIN
PEDLARS GENERAL STORE AND CAFE
PIPPA SMALL
TEMPERLEY LONDON

NOTTING HILL

KENSINGTON

LUCKY SEVEN

THE TIN SHED

WORMWOOD
THE JACKSONS
THE RUM KITCHEN

N

PORTOBELLO ROAD MARKETS

PEDLARS GENERAL STORE AND CAFE

All Saints

0   50 m

HONEY JAM

BOOKS FOR COOKS

COUVERTURE & THE GARBSTORE

TEMPERLEY LONDON

DVF

MATCHES

ILOVEGORGEOUS

LUTYENS & RUBINSTEIN

GAIL'S ARTISAN BAKERY

OTTOLENGHI

PENELOPE CHILVERS

LEDBURY ROAD

PIPPA SMALL

ADMIRAL VERNON ANTIQUES ARCADE

WILD AT HEART

EMMA HOPE

WOLF & BADGER

SWEATY BETTY

BEACH BLANKET BABYLON

AIME

FARA KIDS

VILLAS

PORTOBELLO GOLD

ALICE'S

NOTTING HILL

Stanley Crescent Garden

TO
THE CROSS, COWSHED & MELT CHOCOLATES (SEE MAP LEFT)

TO
KENSINGTON CHURCH & HIGH STREETS (NOT SHOWN ON MAP)

24

1.

COUVERTURE & THE GARBSTORE

188 Kensington Park Road,
W11 2ES
020 7229 2178,
couvertureandthegarbstore.com
Mon–Sat 10am–6pm,
Sun 12–5pm

In this light, airy former townhouse, previously home to a timber yard, husband and wife team Ian Paley and Emily Dyson (daughter of genius vacuum inventor James), have an impressive mix of niche independent labels, all with an authentic, intuitive feel. Their own Garbstore collection for men (where Ian's inspired by reimagined post-WWII influences) and Emily's keen eye for beautiful, interesting pieces for women, kids and home, are placed alongside designers from New York to Berlin, Japan to Belgium. There's a new fragrance line too, No Chemicals, which is hand-blended in limited quantities in Paris from the natural essential oils of frankincense, lavender, ginger, rose and cedar wood, echoing the sense of exclusivity and individuality of the store.

2.

COWSHED

119 Portland Road, W11 4LN
020 7078 1944,
cowshedonline.com
Mon–Tues 9am–8pm (cafe 8:30am–3pm), Wed–Fri 9am–9pm (cafe 8:30am–3pm), Sat 9am–7pm (cafe 9am–3pm), Sun 10am–5pm (cafe 10am–3pm)

Being on holiday is sometimes the only time to do any pampering – and Cowshed is a great place to do it. Part of the Soho House group, its first ever spa was in an actual cow shed, at its Somerset country retreat Babington House, where the Cowshed botanical beauty product range and treatments were born, inspired by ingredients growing in the estate's walled garden. Luxury is key here – comfortable, oversized recliner chairs, your own retro TV and machiattos (or wine) on tap. Switch off and *relax*, soaking up those natural essences whilst a therapist gives you a scalp massage, or try the Slender Cow scrub and massage for all over body rejuvenation. For ladies and gents.

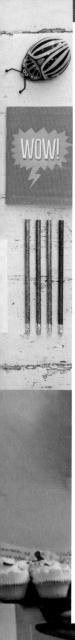

3.
THE CROSS

141 Portland Road, W11 4LR
020 7727 6760,
thecrossshop.co.uk
Mon–Sat 10am–6pm

There can only be a feeling
of joy when crossing the
colourful threshold of The
Cross, filled to the brim
like an ethnic bazaar with
everything chic and stylish
you can imagine from
clothing to fragrance, gifts to
homewares. In its 20 years
as one of Notting Hill's most
cherished top shopping
spots, owner Sam Robinson
has always championed
off-radar labels alongside
long-established brands
like Dosa and Queene &
Belle – here you'll find woven
beach bags with laid-back
hippie mantras, digital
printed cashmere, Edina
Ronay tea dresses and
embroidered tunics. There
are soft toys, cute jumpers,
screen prints and games for
kids, cushions, throws and
candles for the home. Being
in here always makes me
feel like I've just arrived on
holiday somewhere warm,
welcoming and exotic.

4.
LEDBURY ROAD

Ledbury Road is a gentle,
tree-lined shopping street far
from Portobello's madding
crowd. Find a little hint of
Parisian chic with French–
Cambodian sisters Val and
Vanda's charming fashion
and lifestyle store **Aimé**.
Pore over velvet trainers
and sparkly sling-back heels
at **Emma Hope**, or the
hottest velvet Chelsea boots,
embroidered cowboy boots
and loafers at **Penelope
Chilvers**. There's groovy
workout gear at **Sweaty
Betty**, hip streetwear
and accessories for men
and women at **Wolf &
Badger**, and the cutest,
sparkliest clothes for kids at
ilovegorgeous (photo 4A).
Speaking of gorgeous, for
grown-up fashion go to
Matches and **DvF**. Finally,
take a break over a raspberry-
swirl meringue and coffee at
Ottolenghi (photo this page
bottom) or luxuriate in plush
surroundings over a Pornstar
Martini at **Beach Blanket
Babylon**. And we hear the
upmarket charity store **Fara
Kids** is ripe for the picking
with local A-listers' littlies'
designer cast-offs.

5.

HONEY JAM
2 Blenheim Crescent, W11 1NN
020 7243 0449,
honeyjam.co.uk
Mon–Sat 10am–6pm,
Sun 11am–4pm

Honey Jam is how you dream a children's toy shop should be. Indeed, it's exactly what owners Honey Bowdrey (Honey) and former model Jasmine Guinness (Jam), with seven children between them, missed from their own childhoods – toyshops crammed to the rafters with colourful, clever and intriguing games, old-fashioned bears and dolls, dressing up clothes (including beautiful fairy dresses), making kits and a charming range of wooden toys. Some are beautifully handcrafted, some are pocket-money-affordable, but all of it has a very appealing nostalgia of going on adventures with Enid Blyton's *Famous Five*.

Rabbit Lamp
£75.00

Made in England for
HONEY JAM
By
Merrythought

Made in England for
JAM
ythought

6.

LUTYENS & RUBINSTEIN

21 Kensington Park Road,
W11 2EU
020 7229 1010,
lutyensrubinstein.co.uk
Mon & Sat 10am–6pm,
Tues–Fri 10am–6.30pm,
Sun 11am–5pm

Every book in Lutyens &
Rubinstein's cosy bookshop
is there because somebody
loves it and recommended it.
Established literary agents
Sarah Lutyens and Felicity
Rubinstein sought the input
of writers, literary colleagues
and friends (young and old) to
discover exactly what kinds of
books they wanted to find on
these shelves – the result is a
wonderful mix of fiction and
coffee table tomes, illustrated
children's books and moving
memoirs. Then there are
L&R's own cup and saucers
etched with favourite literary
sayings, canvas tote bags,
jars of honey (from beehives
kept just around the corner on
Westbourne Grove), cards and
gift wrap. The book-inspired
art and limited-edition prints
are almost as brilliant as the
well-considered opinions of
the knowledgeable staff.

The Communist
Manifesto

Karl Marx &
Friedrich Engels

PEDLARS GENERAL STORE AND CAFE

128 Talbot Road, W11 1JA
020 7727 7799, pedlars.co.uk
Mon–Sat 8am–6pm,
Sun 10am–5pm

Pedlars started out as a mail order clothing catalogue, operating from the Scottish highlands by founders Charlie and Caroline Gladstone, until one day Charlie was bitten by the vintage bug and the bright, breezy, upbeat Pedlars was born. It is filled with old finds from their journeys around the brocantes of France, and contemporary design with an emphasis on British-made craftsmanship. The couple's passion for the great outdoors means the shop brims with things to help you have fun: board games and rope lanyards, dog whistles and campfire cookers, portable espresso machines and fireside-scented candles, Swiss Army shovels and candles smelling of fresh mountain air. Oh, and they serve stonkingly good coffee.

8.

PIPPA SMALL

201 Westbourne Grove,
W11 2SB
020 7792 1292,
pippasmall.com
Mon–Sat 11am–6pm

You'll be captivated by Pippa Small's ethnic (and ethically) inspired jewellery designs. The stones, from pyrite, tourmaline, opal, amethyst and moonstone to quartz and labradorite, are often rough-cut and intriguingly flawed, in shapes like flowers, stars and raincloud droplets. Each piece tells a story of the places Pippa goes to source stones and inspiration – she works with tribal and Indigenous craftspeople on collections that provide work and income to help their communities survive (from Botswana and Rwanda to Afghanistan's Turquoise Mountain; she's also a human rights ambassador for Survival International). Some pieces are affordable enough for an impulse buy, others might need to be reserved for the next dream purchase.

TEMPERLEY LONDON

6–7 Colville Mews, W11 2DA
020 7229 7957,
temperleylondon.com
Mon–Fri 10am–6pm & Thurs
until 7pm, Sat 11am–6pm

- -

Designer Alice Temperley, and her collection of elaborately embroidered and often dramatically printed clothing, scarves, shoes and wedding dresses, are the personification of British bohemian rock chic. A free, creative spirit embodies her clothes, with each season's collection very much reflecting the way Alice herself likes to dress. Long layers of floating silk and lace one day, pinstripe suits and trilbies the next. Tucked away down a cobbled mews with its facade emblazoned with a Union Jack flag (she also has a store in Mayfair), browse the rails while being served tea in proper cups and enjoy the sense of carefree harmony filling the air. If you can't stretch the budget to a dress, take home a beautifully embroidered scarf, clutch or cushion or set of heavenly scented candles.

10.
BOOKS FOR COOKS

4 Blenheim Crescent,
W11 1NN
020 7221 1992,
booksforcooks.com
Tues–Sat 10am–6pm

The ultimate foodie mecca, Books for Cooks' shelves heave and sigh with every cookbook you can imagine: new, old, rare and out of print, fun and frivolous, serious and scientific. Owned by husband and wife team Rosie Kindersley and French chef Eric Treuille, Eric oversees and teaches many of the workshops. Cooking classes and talks are held regularly and the shop is always infused with the tantalising smells of new dishes being cooked and tested, with ingredients sourced from the nearby Portobello market, and served to customers for lunch. Book ahead for one of their very hands-on workshops, taken by authors of books stocked instore, complemented with a glass of wine from Eric's own French biodynamic vineyard.

11.
KENSINGTON CHURCH AND HIGH STREETS

From Notting Hill Gate Station, it's a leisurely 15–20 minute walk south to High Street, wandering along beautiful Church Street. Check out local spots like chef Sally Clarke's long-standing **Clarke's** restaurant, a west London institution (and over the road, she's opened a deli selling her famous bread and chocolates). Admire **The Churchill Arms** (photo this page, bottom), festooned with hanging pots of flowers, and visit **The Rowley Gallery** and antique shop **The Lacquer Chest** (photo 11C). Detour down Holland Street to see showbiz photographer **Richard Young**, the design destination **Willer** (photo 11B) and fashion boutique **Musa** (photo 11A). When you reach High Street, marvel at the magnificent 1872 neo-Gothic **St Mary Abbots Church** and the late 19th century **Barkers of Kensington** building, in its heyday a glorious department store, today home to the city's largest **Whole Foods Market**, complete with top floor food hall. High Street favourites include **M&S** (and its food hall) and bookshop **Waterstones**. Sporty bods will like **Altimus** and **Snow + Rock**.

MELT CHOCOLATES

6 Clarendon Road, W11 3AA
020 8354 4504,
meltchocolates.com
Mon–Sat 8.30am–6.30pm,
Sun 11am–5pm

Bars flavoured with popcorn, peanut butter or toast and marmalade lined up in bright rainbow-hued boxes along ceiling height shelves, hot choc blocks on sticks, scoopfuls of white chocolate raspberry and mint fresh bonbons, daily made coconut squares – there is no end to the chocoholic delights at Melt. Everything is made on site so the first thing that greets you is the sweet, bitter, earthy cocoa-enriched delicious scent of chocolate being melted, tempered and transformed into morsels from heaven. Founder Louise Nason's elegant touch with mid-century modern furniture and lighting against the store's clean, white minimalist backdrop makes it a great place to stop for a choccy treat, coffee, and to watch the chefs at play. They have another store on Ledbury Road.

13.

GAIL'S ARTISAN BAKERY

138 Portobello Road, W11 2DZ
020 7460 0766,
gailsbread.co.uk
Mon–Fri 7am–7pm, Sat
7am–8pm, Sun 8am–8pm

This good-looking bakery and cafe is part of a small but growing chain of bakeries around the city – come here for a strong coffee and energy boost before scouring the hundreds of stalls lining Portobello Road. Gail's bakes around 30 different types of bread fresh each day – including a variety of different sourdough loaves, flavoured with olives, caramelised garlic, honey, almonds and walnuts; there's even a dark French version that's lovingly made from a 15-year-old yeast starter. Flaky croissant dough makes light-as-air cinnamon buns or moreish sausage rolls; at lunch there are big bowls of fresh, healthy salads with roasted veggies, marinated chicken or fish, herbs and pulses, quinoa and lentils. For the sweet tooth, it's impossible to resist the zingy lemon drizzle cake, rich, intense pecan chocolate brownie or fluffy, fruity friands.

14.

LUCKY SEVEN

127 Westbourne Park Road, W2 5QL
020 7727 6771,
lucky7london.co.uk
Mon–Thurs 12–11pm, Fri 12–11.30pm, Sat 9am–11.30pm, Sun 9am–10.30pm

---

Lucky Seven is my family's favourite happy place; a tucked-away local gem owned by Tom Conran (he also owns Crazy Homies next door and highly-regarded gastropub The Cow two blocks down). We dive into a deep green leather booth, admire the kitsch American diner memorabilia on the walls (life-sized models of Ronald McDonald characters, 60s psychedelic art), and order greedily: the double-decker, fully loaded High Roller for him, the New Kalifornian (with bacon and guacamole) for me, fries and slaw on the side. For the kids, perfect-sized burgers, rich, thick milkshakes, and a proper banana split for afters. It's simple, fast, tasty and lifts the spirits (on weekends they do piles of buttermilk pancakes and huevos rancheros for breakfast too).

13.

14.

14.

221

There's lots to discover around Portobello: Asian flavours at **E&O** (Blenheim Crescent) and luxe take-away fare at **The Grocer on Elgin**. On All Saints Road, eat at **Wormwood**, drink at **The Rum Kitchen** and shop for quirky fashion at **The Jacksons**. On Kensington Park Road, there's distinctive fashion at **Merchant Archive** and **One Vintage**; and take home pretty iced biscuits in decorative tins from **Biscuiteers**. On Westbourne Grove there's a holiday vibe to fashion at **Heidi Klein**, **Melissa Odabash** and **Olebar Brown**; gobstopper jewels at **Dinny Hall** and **Ben Day** (3 Lonsdale Road); and beautiful blooms at **Wild At Heart**. On Portland Road, visit **Summerill & Bishop** for heavenly kitchenware.

Kensington Palace (Kensington Gardens, W8 4PX, hrp.org.uk) is Prince William's official family residence and home to a collection dedicated to Queen Victoria. Enjoy afternoon tea at the **Orangery** (orangerykensingtonpalace. co.uk), then take the kids to the **Diana, Princess of Wales Memorial Playground**.

Holland Park's gardens include the **Kyoto Gardens** with waterfalls and ponds of carp, the award-winning children's **Ecology Centre** (rbkc. gov.uk), and the **Design Museum** (designmuseum.org) from late 2016.

The Museum of Brands (111–117 Lancaster Road, W11 1QT, museumofbrands.com) is a cornucopia of 12,000 items of retro packaging and advertising.

For a fascinating insight into Victorian-era decoration, travel and collecting, don't miss **Leighton House** (12 Holland Park Road, W14 8LZ, rbkc.gov.uk), with gilded domed ceilings, tiled walls and floors and a charming winter painting studio.

NOTTING HILL LOCAL RECOMMENDS

Notting Hill local **Alice Temperley** opened her first shop here in 2001.

Alice's

(86 Portobello Road): Established in 1887, and still run in the family, Alice's has an eclectic selection of British memorabilia, bric-a-brac, old-fashioned toys, taxidermy and travelling trunks (I dream of owning this shop, for obvious namesake reasons!).

Portobello Gold

(95–97 Portobello Road): I like the nice romantic tucked-away bits at the back and settling in for a drink and live music on a Sunday night.

Santo

(299 Portobello Road): The best Mexican place for margaritas (in seven variations) and fresh, mouth-watering quesadillas and ceviche, with fun music nights on Friday and Saturday.

Portobello Road Markets: I've been a regular since I moved to London as a textiles student – I have always loved collecting stuff, I like anything that shines. It's good for vintage clothes (only on Friday) and on Saturday mornings I love to mooch around **Admiral Vernon Antiques Arcade** (141–149 Portobello Road) for jewellery, interesting fabrics, crockery and objects for the home. Best to go early.

One of a Kind

(259 Portobello Road): Brilliant for vintage men's clothing (particularly denim jeans), plus inspiring shoes and bags.

Electric Diner

(191 Portobello Road): I come here for the best breakfasts. Eggs any style, gruyere cheese omelettes, waffles with jam and cream. Great fresh cold-pressed juices, too.

The Tin Shed

(33 All Saints Road): Bustling with fashion people, and serving a perfect all-day brunch menu.

At the heart of North Kensington is Golborne Road, with its wonderful street-side stalls, heaving with fresh produce or delectable take-away dishes like Moroccan-spiced sea bass. It's great for shopping too (*see page 234*), with a mix of vintage furniture, hip fashion and accessories shops.

Trellick Tower (*see page 234*) is the major landmark and from many vantage points around west London it's a strangely comforting one – its 31 storeys of Brutalist geometry rising high above the Westway (one of London's main road arteries), always helps give a sense of bearing to where one is in the city.

Kensal Green Cemetery

LADBROKE GROVE
ST JOHN'S TERRACE
HARROW ROAD
DROOP STREET
MAPLE WALK
SIXTH AVENUE
ROWAN WALK

Grand Union Canal

TOM DIXON & THE DOCK KITCHEN

LADBROKE GROVE
CANAL CLOSE
WAY
CANAL
KENSAL ROAD
WEST

LADBROKE GROVE

Heathrow Connect/Express & Great Western Railway

SOUTHERN ROW
LADBROKE
ROW

ADMIRAL MEWS

BARLBY ROAD
GROVE

TO MAP RIGHT
(VIA LADBROKE GROVE)

NORTH KENSINGTON

SHOP
1 ALLY CAPELLINO
2 HONEST JON'S
3 LES COUILLES DU CHIEN
4 RELLIK

24 JUN 8OT6

17

SHOP AND EAT
TOM DIXON & THE DOCK KITCHEN, PORTOBELLO DOCK
EAT
PIZZA EAST
SNAPS + RYE

RELLIK

MANCHESTER DRIVE

APPLEFORD ROAD

GOLBORNE GARDENS

HAZLEWOOD CRESCENT

ADAIR

KENSINGTON

ROAD

Meanwhile Gardens

GOLBORNE ROAD

Trellick Tower

Heathrow Connect/Express & Great Western Railway

SOUTHAM STREET

WEST THIRTY SIX

ELKSTONE

WORNINGTON

ROAD

N

ROAD

TELFORD ROAD

ROAD

ROAD

ST ERVANS

ACKLAM ROAD

FARADAY

LARA BOHINC

LISBOA

CAFÉ OPORTO

LES COUILLES DU CHIEN

0   50 m

MEWS

FEZ

OLLIE & BOW

ROAD

ARBON INTERIORS

GOLBORNE ROAD MARKET

KOKON TO ZAI

PORTOBELLO

OLD PONY

MUNRO

JANE BOURVIS

WORNINGTON

MORGAN ROAD

ERNO DECO

SNAPS + RYE

ORCHARD

CLOSE

GOLBORNE DELI

J & M DAVIDSON

ROAD

ALLY CAPELLINO

BEVINGTON

CLOSE

ROAD

GOLBORNE MEWS

PIZZA EAST

MALVERN

CHESTERTON ROAD

GALICIA

BEVINGTON ROAD

CLOSE

PORTOBELLO

ST JOSEPHS

Portobello Road Arts Project-North Wall

BLAGROVE

ROAD

SAINT

CLOSE

NORTH KENSINGTON

RADDINGTON ROAD

ROAD

LAWRENCE

ACKLAM

ROAD

ROAD

A40

TERRACE

GARDENS

ROAD

WESTWAY

Hammersmith & City line

LADBROKE GROVE

TO TOM DIXON & THE DOCK KITCHEN (SEE MAP LEFT)

OXFORD

HONEST JON'S

ACKLAM ROAD

Circle line

CAMBRIDGE GARDENS

225

ALLY CAPELLINO

312 Portobello Road, W10 5RU
020 8964 1022,
allycapellino.co.uk
Mon–Sat 11am–6pm,
Sun 11am–5pm

Ally Capellino, real name Alison Lloyd, has long held an enviable cult following for her pared-back, understated, graceful but imminently functional satchels, totes, bucket bags, purses and rucksacks. Working with the softest leathers, hard-wearing nylon and waxed cotton (all made in Britain), there are also accessories like neat little wool cycle caps by This is Cambridge, leather glasses chains and dog leads. Her overnight holdall is a classic; 'Frank', one of her most iconic waxed cotton backpacks, and a hit with cyclists, is updated every season. Collaborations have included bags and accessories for Apple, the Ace Hotel and The Tate. These are pieces for those who value timelessness and quality with longevity.

HONEST JON'S

278 Portobello Road, W10 5TE
020 8969 9822,
honestjons.com
Mon–Sat 10.30am–6pm,
Sun 11am–5pm

With the download generation comes the risk of losing such inspirational record stores as Honest Jon's. It's been on the London music scene since the 1970s, but given fresh impetus with the initiation of its own label (run in conjunction with Blur frontman and solo artist Damon Albarn). The music choice here is eclectic – a mecca for die-hard fans of jazz, blues and reggae, but you can also hunt out rare (and reprint) vinyl and CDs of gospel and soul, and what the label dubs 'outernational' grooves, encompassing the Ethiopiques to the romantic mornas of Cape Verde. New artists under the label include electronica composer Laurel Halo and Glaswegian folk harmonists The Crying Lion.

3.

LES COUILLES DU CHIEN

65 Golborne Road, W10 5NP
020 8968 0099,
lescouillesduchien.com
Mon–Sat 9.30am–5pm

Expect the unexpected at
Jerome Dodd's treasure
trove of vintage furniture,
lighting and accessories.
Les Couilles du Chien ('the
dog's bollocks') has been
a stalwart of the Golborne
Road antiques scene for over
25 years. Here nothing is too
weird or wonderful – you'll
find natural history curiosities
like taxidermy frogs and
lobsters alongside a 1950s
Italian chrome magazine rack;
tassel-fringed 19th century
salon chairs vie for attention
next to a floor lamp made of
deer antlers; and anatomy
maps hang by specimens of
vivid blue Ulysses butterflies.

4.

RELLIK

8 Golborne Road, W10 5NW
020 8962 0089,
relliklondon.co.uk
Tues–Sat 10am–6pm

Fiona Stuart, Claire Stansfield
and Steven Phillip are the
trio behind Rellik, one of
the fashion world's key
destinations for inspiration.
Famed names like uber stylist
Katie Grand, designer John
Galliano, Bella Freud, Kate
Moss, Chloe Sevigny and
Kylie Minogue have rifled
the rails in this jewel of a
shop resting in the shadow
of the Trellick Tower. Come
here for clothing, accessories
and shoes by Comme des
Garçons, Yohji Yamamoto and
Issey Miyake; vintage Yves
Saint Laurent, Alaïa, and
Courrèges are highly sought-
after; if you're lucky to spot
a Thea Porter or Ossie Clark,
just grab it (these sell in
seconds); and there's always
timeless Brit pieces from the
likes of Vivienne Westwood
and Alexander McQueen.

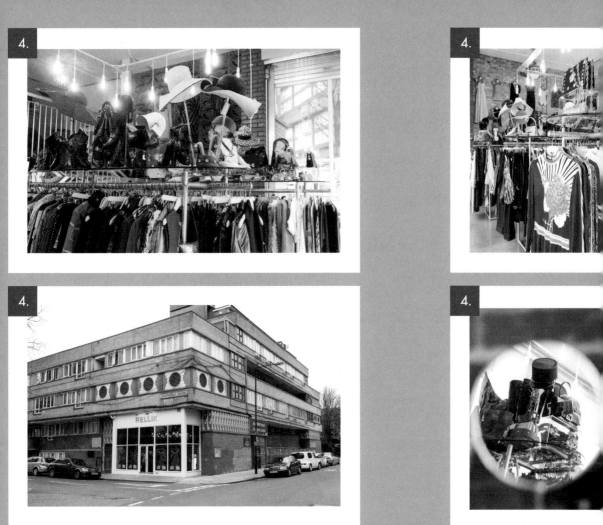

4.

4.

4.

3.

Les Couilles du Chien

5.

TOM DIXON & THE DOCK KITCHEN, PORTOBELLO DOCK

Portobello Docks, 342–344
Ladbroke Grove, W10 5BU
Tom Dixon (020 7183 9737,
tomdixon.net): Mon–Sat
10am–6pm, Sun 11am–5pm;
The Dock Kitchen (020 8962
1610, dockkitchen.co.uk):
Mon–Sat 12–2.30pm &
7–9.30pm, Sun 12–3pm

- -

Designer Tom Dixon moved
his studio and showroom
into a converted Victorian
wharf building, and teamed
up with chef Stevie Parle
(ex River Cafe, Moro and
Petersham Nurseries) to
create an inspiring place to
eat, drink and shop. Stevie's
menus change with the
seasons – fresh *langoustines*
flown in from France one
day, sumac roasted guinea
fowl the next. His global
palate draws inspiration from
Thailand to Turkey. He also
hosts themed nights revolving
around a place, an ingredient
or a visiting chef. Downstairs,
in between Tom's iconic
winged armchairs and mirror
ball lights, you'll find smart
accessories in brass and
copper like the Brew range of
coffee accessories, organically
beaten Bash bowls, and
exquisitely scented candles
(take home 'London', infused
with the smell of red brick,
crocuses, nettles, and the salt
of the Thames).

6.

PIZZA EAST

310 Portobello Road, W10 5TA
020 8969 4500,
pizzaeast.com
Mon–Thurs 8am–11.30pm,
Fri–Sat 8am–12am, Sun
8am–10.30pm

You know a place is good when it heaves from morning to night with local west Londoners. Spread across two floors of a restored Georgian pub, Pizza East is a bright, sunny, welcoming and laid-back place, serving wood-fired pizzas – the crispy pork belly or burrata, aubergine (eggplant) and pesto are recommended – boards of antipasti (to eat in or take-away) and comfort staples like oven-baked mac'n'cheese, served up with cocktails like the Cynar Mule (Italian botanical bitter liqueur with Jamaican run, ginger syrup and lime). Even at breakfast, it seems wrong to say no to a Mimosa over baked eggs with mushrooms, spinach and tallegio.

7

SNAPS + RYE

93 Golborne Road, W10 5NL
020 8964 3004,
snapsandrye.com
Tues–Wed 8am–6pm, Thurs–Sat
8am–11pm, Sun 10am–6pm

My favourite Saturday
morning treat is heading to
Snaps + Rye for a light and
lovely breakfast. Smooth,
rich coffee teamed with
one of the many daily
Smørrebrød open sandwich
variations (although I find it
hard to bypass the house-
cured salmon with sweet
sliced radish on light, nutty
rye bread). It's a relaxing,
calming escape, decked out
in Nordic pale woods and
white walls, opened in 2014
by Danish–English locals Kell
and Jacqueline Skott. They
pair Danish flavours with
fresh organic and sustainable
ingredients – specialties
include Baked rarebit (rye
bread soaked in malt beer
with eggs and Danish Gamle
Ole Cheese), the Full Danish
(complete with liquorice
syrup and Bloody Viking
Ketchup), *Fiskefrikadellar* (fish
cake using what's in season),
and *Gammeldags Æblekage*
(a Danish layer caked with
apple compote and cinnamon
brandy crumble).

I love spending a few hours wandering up and down Golborne Road, browsing the chic coats and hand-stitched leather handbags at **J&M Davidson**, sculptural jewellery at **Lara Bohinc**, **Jane Bourvis's** ethereal vintage laces, silks and embroideries, old-fashioned toys at **Old Pony**, and hipster fashion meets quirky homewares at **Kokon to Zai**. Find crazy things like ceramic parrots at **Arbon Interiors** and vibrant Moroccan ceramics at **Fez**. For great pub grub, head to **West Thirty Six** for the rotisserie chicken and rack of ribs.

Designed by Ernö Goldfinger in 1972 as a radical solution for high-rise social housing, legend has it that the **Trellick Tower** so incensed Bond author Ian Fleming he named an arch-villain after the architect. The block's history is checkered with tales of crime and unhappiness but today it stands as a symbol of great pride and joy. For architecture fans, although outside this precinct, it's worth visiting Goldfinger's home in Hampstead, **2 Willow Road** (2 Willow Road, NW3 1TH, nationaltrust.org.uk; bookings essential).

From Tom Dixon's Dock (see page 230), it's a two-minute walk along Harrow Road to **Kensal Green Cemetery** (Harrow Road, W10 4RA, kensalgreencemetery. com) where you can pay respects to the likes of revered 19th century engineer Isambard Kingdom Brunel, writers Anthony Trollope and William Makepeace Thackeray, and members of the nobility, including the children of George III, and the servants of Queen Victoria.

Fiona Stuart co-founded vintage store Rellik in 1999.

Lisboa

(57 Golborne Road): New coffee shops always open on Golborne and Portobello roads, but Lisboa is the granddaddy of them all, making their own mouth-melting Portuguese 'patel de nata' custard tarts (go early while they're still warm and not yet sold out). **Café Oporto** at number 62 comes a close second.

Golborne Road Market: The market
is on a Friday or Saturday. Cruise the kerbside for bric-a-brac, flowers and fresh fish amongst the great food stalls.

Golborne Deli (100 Golborne
Road): It's busy for a reason. Fast and friendly, it makes the best paninis.

Galicia (323 Portobello Road): By
night this is a wonderful Spanish tapas bar, a long-standing Notting Hill fixture. The food is authentic, delicious and very good value.

Ollie & Bow (69 Golborne Road):
Ollie's is full of lights, chairs, soft furnishings and objects to love. I also always take a peek too in **Erno Deco** (328 Portobello Road).

London is big but it's easy to get around, with plenty of transport options. Visit **Transport for London** (TfL): tfl.gov.uk.

TICKETS

Use an Oyster card ticket or debit/credit card for all Underground, bus, District Light Rail (DLR), London Overground, TfL Rail, most National Rail services and River Bus services (MBNA Thames Clippers).

Oyster cards can be purchased online to arrive at your hotel ahead of your visit. You can top up money on an Oyster card at any time, in a station or online, which allows you to touch in and out (capped at a maximum day rate no matter how many journeys you take). Children under 11 travel free (when accompanied by a fare-paying adult), children 11–15 years pay half adult rates. Or use a debit or credit card to tap in and out (same day capping rates apply as an Oyster card).

TRAIN

The Underground (Tube) operates in central and some parts of greater London, and the Overground forms an Outer London orbital network.

Underground (Tube)

The 'Tube' is a breeze and by far the best way to navigate the city. There are ten main lines, clearly shown on the iconic tube map. A Night Tube service runs 24 hours on the Jubilee, Victoria, Central, Northern and Piccadilly lines; it will be rolled out for the other lines between 2017 and 2021.

To work out which way you're going, find the station you need, look to see what line it's on, and what the line's end destination will be to tell you whether you need to travel north or south bound. A station or platform attendant will always be happy to help.

Tube safety and etiquette

Allow passengers off first by standing to the left or right of the opening doors.

Don't race to catch a Tube as you'll risk injury or being separated from travelling companions. There's always another Tube coming – they are frequent.

Always carry a bottle of water with you as the Tube can get very hot.

If you don't feel well, wait until you reach the next train platform before pulling the emergency cord; you can seek help from a platform attendant.

Don't be offended if no one engages with you – but take heart, they'll happily chat on a bus.

At Tube stations, keep left to walk up an escalator, keep right to enjoy an easier ride up (some Tube lines are hundreds of metres down and the escalator rides are long).

Overground

There are six Overground train routes: Richmond/Clapham Junction to Stratford, Watford Junction to Euston, Gospel Oak to Barking, Highbury & Islington to West Croydon/Clapham Junction, Liverpool Street to Enfield Town, Cheshunt (via Seven Sisters) and Chingford, Romford to Upminster.

Airport express trains

Heathrow Express from Paddington station (heathrowexpress.com), **Stansted**

Express from Liverpool Street station (standstedexpress.com), **Gatwick Express** from Victoria station (gatwickexpress.com), **City Airport** via DLR. Pay either online or on the station platform before you travel (it will cost more to buy tickets onboard).

BUSES

Buses are a wonderful way to see London and gain your bearings, with a network of bus operators reaching every part of the city. Key routes for tourist spots and sightseeing are:

10: King's Cross via Oxford Circus to High Street Kensington

23: Westbourne Gove via Oxford Circus and Aldwych to Liverpool Street

74: Baker Street via Marble Arch and Knightsbridge to Putney

9: Aldwych via Hyde Park Corner to High Street Kensington

73: Victoria via Marble Arch, Oxford Circus, Kings Cross to Stoke Newington

12: Oxford Circus via Piccadilly and Westminster to Dulwich

390: Notting Hill Gate via Oxford Circus and Euston to Archway

14: Putney via Fulham, South Kensington, Chelsea, Piccadilly to Tottenham Court Road

Bus Tours

There are various London sightseeing bus tour companies, including themed tours like 'London by Night', and many will allow you to hop off so you can enjoy an attraction, and then hop back on again. **Visit London** (visitlondon.com) lists all tours.

WALKING

We've all made the mistake of catching the Tube from Piccadilly to Leicester Square, only to realise it's a short walk, and you'll just see so much more on foot.

Visit London (visitlondon.com) lists walking tours, **TfL** (tfl.gov.uk) has a great journey planner, or download five great walks from **Walk London** (walklondon.com). For walking the beautiful Royal parks, download **The Diana Princess of Wales Memorial Walk** route map (royalparks.org.uk).

CAR CLUBS

If you just fancy driving around the city, car clubs can take the stress out of parking permits, insurance and pricey car rental agreements. Sign up in advance, pay a minimal membership fee, download the app to find your nearest car, and away you go. You'll pay by the hour.

Check with your travel insurance about whether your licence from home covers car hire. The car clubs will also have information about accepted licences and whether you are liable for the central London Congestion Charge, easily payable online.

Try **Zipcar** (zipcar.co.uk), **City Car Club** (citycarclub.co.uk), and **E-Car** (e-carclub.org).

You drive on the left hand side of the road in the UK and Northern Ireland (unlike in the rest of Europe, including southern Ireland, where you drive on the right).

Read up on driving tips, from country to country, at **AA** (theaa.com).

CYCLING

Santander Cycles or 'Boris' bikes are a great way to see the city. Access is via the docking station or app (tfl.gov.uk/modes/cycling/santander-cycles). You'll have to pay a small bike access fee and the first 30 minutes hire is free (then charged at 30-minute intervals). You can only hire a bike for less than 24 hours.

There are a number of cycle tour companies that will provide bikes, safety kit and experienced tour guides – try **The London Bicycle Tour Company** (londonbicycle.com) or **BrakeAway Bike Tours** (biketouroflondon.com).

Cycling safety

London is an often chaotic and impatient city, and the development of cycle paths is ongoing.

Beware of blind spots around large vehicles and lorries, so stay well behind them.

Stick to cycle paths and back streets rather than main thoroughfares; walk across busy junctions and intersections.

Wear reflective clothing and accessories; avoid wearing all black.

Don't wear headphones or use your mobile phone. Be alert at all times.

TAXIS

Black Cabs

London is famous for its fleet of black cabs and the drivers who have had to complete an exhaustive test called The Knowledge, testing them on every London street and route.

It's safe to hail a black cab on the street (look for a yellow light to see if it's free); you'll also find black cab ranks outside tube stations and major hotels. A hotel doorman will always be happy to help you find a cab.

Payment is in cash – generally rounded up with a £1–2 tip. Some cabs take credit cards, but ask before you hop in.

Pay heed to any requests not to eat or drink in a cab, don't put your feet up on the folding down footstools and wear a seatbelt at all times.

Download the **Hailo app** to help find and book the nearest black cab to you.

Mini Cabs

Mini cabs offer an alternative to catching black cabs, but be sure to only book one that has been fully licensed by Transport for London. Book by phone or via an app; never accept a lift from someone who approaches you on the street offering a mini cab service, especially outside a nightclub. If you are ever in doubt about a driver, even after arriving safely at your destination, do not hesitate to call the police to make a complaint. The TfL and Metropolitan Police work very closely to monitor mini cabs to ensure everyone's safety.

Addison Lee (addisonlee.com) provides a reputable licensed mini cab company. Payment can be in advance via credit card (arranged when booking online, over the phone or via the app) or by cash on arrival.

Thames Clippers

A scenic and leisurely way to travel is by water, from Putney to North Greenwich, via the Thames Clipper service (thamesclippers.com). Stopping at handy sightseeing spots like Millbank for Tate Britain, Waterloo for the London Eye, Bankside for Tate Modern and London Bridge for the City. Departures are every 20 minutes (on weekends the service travels to and from the London Eye to Woolwich only).

ABOUT THE AUTHOR

Journalist and contributing editor Fiona McCarthy has been based in London from her native Perth since 1993. As a penniless wannabe journalist, the cheapest and easiest way to get around was by foot – serendipitously providing the perfect opportunity to discover every nook and cranny of such a big, higgledy-piggledy city.

With a keen passion for seeking out unusual and intriguing places, particularly those off the beaten track, and a love of telling people's stories, for almost two decades, Fiona has divided her time between writing on fashion, beauty, design, interiors, food and travel for all the British major newspapers (including *The Mail on Sunday's YOU Magazine*, *Stella* and *Telegraph* magazine, and *The Sunday Times' Style*) and lifestyle glossies (including *Living Etc*, *Elle Decoration*, *House & Garden* and *Red*).

Fiona is the London Editor for *Vogue Living* and regularly contributes to *The Australian's WISH* magazine. She has also co-authored *A Living Space* and *Every Room Tells A Story* with interior designer and hotelier Kit Kemp.

Fiona lives in a vertiginous Victorian terrace house in the leafy area of Maida Vale with her architect husband and two children, in a perpetual state of DIY and chaos.

ACKNOWLEDGEMENTS

From Fiona

Thank you to my family, Mike, Ellie-Rose and Sandy, for their patience, enthusiasm and encouragement in all things, always. I would never have found my momentum without Georgia Allright (picture research) and Gabby Ritchie (additional photography) and Claire Lusher (fact checker). An enormous debt of gratitude to all at Hardie Grant, in particular Melissa Kayser, Marg Bowman, Alison Proietto, Alice Barker, Emily Maffei, Michelle Mackintosh and Megan Ellis in Australia, and Stephen King and Kate Pollard in London. Visually, we couldn't have produced this book without the generous support of everyone featured; thank you so much for all your support, it has meant everything to me. But most importantly, this book is the culmination of two decades living, working and making the most of this big, wonderful city, thanks entirely to the support, generosity and insight of my wonderful friends, who hail from all nations, careers and backgrounds; and the thousands of PRs, chefs, shop owners, designers and bartenders who have shared with me their visions, passions and talents. Thanks particularly to Craig Markham and Paula Fitzherbert, without whom my London life would definitely not be the same. So it's a great thrill to be able to share all of this with all of you.

The publisher would like to acknowledge the following individuals and organisations:

Editorial manager
Marg Bowman

Project manager
Alison Proietto

Editor
Alice Barker

Cartography
Emily Maffei

Design
Michelle Mackinstosh

Layout
Megan Ellis

Index
Max McMaster

Pre-press
Megan Ellis, Splitting Image

Photography credits

Half title page Jo Loves (Andrew Meredith)

Title page Duck & Rice (Ed Reeve)

Contents pages Charlene Mullen; Paperchase (Gabby Ritchie)

The roundel and other transport symbols used on maps © Transport for London

The following images are © Gabby Ritchie 23, 25, 27 (5B, C, F), 36, 37, 43, 48 (top), 49, 53, 60 (bottom), 62 (bottom), 63 (7), 113, 119, 143, 172, 209 (4, 4A), 214, 215, 216 (top), 217 (10), 220 (bottom), 221 (middle & bottom), 228 (bottom), 229 (4), 235

Other images x–xi Oliver Grenaa; 4 (bottom) & 5 (3A, B, C, D) Simon Brown; 9 Keiko Oikawa; 10, 11 (7A), 12 (bottom), 13 (8) Carol Sachs; 13 (9) Helen Cathcart; 14 (bottom), 15 (11) Simon Brown; 16 Annabel Kirland; 28 Jamie Orlando Smith (top), Darren Chung (bottom); 29 (6A) Paul Raeside; 34 (top) David Butler; 35 (2) Stephen Morris; 38 Patricia Niven; 40–1 (6) Nikolas Koenig; 46–7 Jason Ingram; 47 (top and bottom right) Jason Ingram, (bottom left) Simon Bevan; 56–7 Paul Raeside; 64, 65 (top left, bottom left and right) Jake Eastham; 65 (middle left and right) David Griffen; 65 (top right) Paul Winch-Furness; 66 Helen Cathcart; 67 Amber Rowlands; 69 Ruth Corney; 74 (top), 75 (3) Amy Murrell, 74 (bottom), 75 (4) Petrina Tinslay; 76 John Carey; 79 Kristen Perers; 84 Yeshen Venema; 85 Ed Reeve; 86–7 Patricia Niven; 88 (top), 89 (bottom) John Carey; 102 (top) Piers Allardyce, (bottom) Matteo Carassale/GAP Photos; 104 (top) Kristen Perers, (bottom) John Carey; 105 (9D, F) Kristen Perers, (9A, B, C) Addie Chinn; 110–11 (1) John Holdship; 112 Sophie Mutevelian; 116–17 John Carey, National Trust Images; 123 (top) Morley von Sternberg, (bottom) Sam Peach; 124 (top) Patricia Niven, (bottom) Rhubarb/Skygarden; 125 (3) Patricia Niven, (4) Rhubarb/ Skygarden; 137 (3B) Andy Martin Architecture; 138 Jamie McGregor Smith; 140 (top), 141 (6B, C) Ruy Teixeira/Waldo Works; 146 Gareth Hacker; 148 (bottom) Paul Winch-Furness; 149 (F) Paul Winch-Furness, (C) James Cant; 158 (bottom) Nick Harvey; 159 (4) Olimpia Castellini; 160 (bottom) Ruy Teixeira/Waldo Works; 162 David Loftus; 181 Richard Johnson; 187 (7C) Andrew Meredith; 189 (bottom) Nick Bailey; 194–5 (1) Inge Clemente; 197 (top left & right, middle & bottom right) Jael Marschner; 199 David Griffen; 200–1 Simon Brown; 206–7 Rachel Manns; 208 (top), 209 (3) Kate Paillat; 210, 211 (middle left) Araminta De Clermont, 211 Errol Rainey; 212 Mia Rose; 216 (bottom) Fuller, Smith & Turner P.L.C.; 218–19 James Bedford; 223 Tomo Brejc; 230–1 Peer Lindgreen/Tom Dixon; 232 Chris Tubbs; 241 (portrait) Simon Brown, (garden) Nick Bailey; 242–3 Greywolf/The Royal Parks

Explore Australia Publishing Pty Ltd
Ground Floor, Building 1, 658 Church Street,
Richmond, VIC 3121

Explore Australia Publishing Pty Ltd is a division of Hardie Grant Publishing Pty Ltd

hardie grant publishing

Published by Explore Australia Publishing Pty Ltd, 2016

Concept, maps, form and design © Explore Australia Publishing Pty Ltd, 2016
Text © Fiona McCarthy, 2016

A Cataloguing-in-Publication entry is available from the catalogue of the National
Library of Australia at www.nla.gov.au

The maps in this publication incorporate data © OpenStreetMap contributors.
OpenStreetMap is made available under the Open Database License:
http://opendatacommons.org/licenses/odbl/1.0/.
Any rights in individual contents of the database are licensed under the
Database Contents License: http://opendatacommons.org/licenses/dbcl/1.0/
See more at: http://opendatacommons.org/licenses/odbl/
Contains OD data © Crown Copyright (2015). For more info visit http://
www.nationalarchives.gov.uk/doc/open-government-licence/version/3/

ISBN-13 9781741174991

10 9 8 7 6 5 4 3 2 1

Printed and bound in China by 1010 Printing International Ltd

www.exploreaustralia.net.au